KOOL-AID AND CARIBOO STEW

KOOL-AID AND CARIBOO STEW

Verena Berger

Library of Congress Control Number:		2011919406
ISBN:	Hardcover	978-1-4653-6139-4
	Softcover	978-1-4653-6138-7
	Ebook	978-1-4653-6140-0

This book was printed in the United States of America.

To order additional copies of this book, contact:
Xlibris Corporation
1-888-795-4274
www.Xlibris.com
Orders@Xlibris.com
102708

Or visit:
www.verenaberger.com

To

Willy

Oliver and Melanie

CONTENTS

Found in Translation

MY ENGLISH KNOWLEDGE was equivalent to that of a country "pumpkin" when I arrived in Vancouver, British Columbia, in May of 1979. I was a young bride from Switzerland. With me I had two suitcases full of clothes and a dictionary.

Being fluent in German and French didn't help me here. Since I could not communicate, my professional education didn't count. I had to start from scratch. Within two weeks, I was hired at McDonald's as a hostess. My responsibilities included wiping tables and picking up the garbage on the parking lot every fifteen minutes. Getting my first job was the easy part.

Not all my language problems could be solved and not all culture gaps bridged with the dictionary.

My physician raised his eyebrows when I requested a "recipe" for my birth control pills. It was not possible to order a "season ticket" for the *Vancouver Sun*. A clerk in the grocery store gave me a "what-the-heck-are-you-talking-about" look when I asked for mayonnaise in a tube.

My new husband, also a Swiss immigrant, and I figured out why the fridge in our rented basement suite was bigger than our shower stall and abandoned our tradition of daily grocery shopping. Instead, we strolled through the aisles at Woodward's Food Floor every Saturday and made it a point to purchase something unknown every week. Among these culinary discoveries was a can of pumpkin. We spooned some out and tasted it; we added sugar and tried again. We cooked it and sampled it hot. We threw it out.

Our first camping trip brought us to Harrison Lake. We watched a young couple launch their boat. The man smiled at us and said, "Nice day, eh?" A few minutes later, Willy, who was more fluent in English than I, told me, we had received an invitation for a boat ride. Unheard-of in Switzerland! At their cabin, our new Canadian friends asked if we wanted to stay for a bonfire and some "hot dogs."

"Heisse Hunde?" I looked shocked at my husband.

He laughed and explained that we were offered "wieners."

Not only don't Canadians eat dog meat, we were also told to give up the search for a juicy horse steak. Canadians don't eat horses, nor is it common for Canadians to cook the tongue, the brain, or the tail from the beef.

Sometimes ignorance was bliss. We nodded and smiled when labeled "DPs," thinking it might be a compliment or a joke at worst. Other times, our obliviousness resulted in embarrassing faux pas.

Once, while reading the menu in a restaurant that offered venison, my husband had the bright idea to inquire for other wild meat. He innocently asked the waitress if she also had beaver and could not figure out why, in an instant, her friendly smile turned into anger.

I guess it wasn't as bad as my worst blooper. The first time I went to the hairdresser, I asked for a "cut-and-blow job."

In 1981, we moved to the Cariboo, onto our own raw, ten-acre lot. Our neighbors showed up, with hammers in hand, for a "work bee." Volunteering was a new concept to us. In the old country, volunteers are hired and get paid small wages. It is from Canadians that we learned to give time and money.

After the birth of our son, my girlfriends organized a baby shower at our house. I panicked. We didn't have running water at our rural property. I prepared our baby's yellow plastic tub and a fresh towel; I filled the canning pot with water and put it on the wood stove. My friends arrived, and to my great surprise and joy, they all brought gifts for our baby. We never got to the "we-experienced-mothers-show-you-how-to-shower-the-baby" part.

With the rural living came the weekly drive to the dump. The first time, we returned with our full load because the sign read "refuse" and we assumed the landfill was full. "Eggs 4 sale" means that eggs can be bought and most likely there are more than four. People do *not* sell garages. Xmas is not X-rated.

Twenty years of living in Canada and some English classes later, we truly feel Canadian. We know "what's up" when the kids have to "jet." We are "sick and tired" when they keep "passing the buck" on neglected chores. We "eavesdrop" on their conversations to find out what is presently and absolutely "rad," but get "worried sick" when we hear too much. We laughed when they suffered the first "hangover" and got "sicker than a dog."

We look forward to the turkey dinner at Thanksgiving, mostly because of the pumpkin pie. Santa Claus is positively jollier than the stern St. Nicklaus. Nevertheless, we first-generation immigrants celebrate Christmas on December 24. My husband volunteers—without pay—on countless committees and I am a dog walker at the SPCA.

Still, it will probably take my husband and me our entire lifetimes to master the whole language and culture barrier. Recently, I sold a story and sent a triumphant e-mail to my writing buddy: "I am flying on cloud seven" followed by an "LOL." She informed me that here, we fly on cloud nine. I don't know what gives us Canadians the right to fly higher than people in Europe, but I intend to find out what it feels like when I sell my next story.

First published in *The Canadian Immigrant*

DESTINATION HONEYMOON

WHILE DRIVING TO the Vancouver airport, June 4, 1979, Willy translated the news from the car radio, "Joe Clark becomes Canada's sixteenth and youngest prime minister."

I didn't care how old our prime minister was. I had my own worries.

We were on our way to Anchorage, then Fairbanks, and finally Barrow, the most northern village in Alaska, the "end of the world," where we planned to get married.

Not having eaten any breakfast, my stomach grumbled. My neck felt as if a string of barbed wire was tightening around it. And my head was pounding over the anxiety of not having a wedding dress. Not that I wanted a formal white dress with all the frills. At this point, any dress would do.

During our first leg of the trip, our flight to Anchorage, I resisted the urge to get up, plant myself in the aisle, and yell to the other passengers, "I am marrying this tall, dark-eyed, handsome prince!" Willy, who sat relaxed by the window, looked up from reading a copy of Maclean's, and gave me a reassuring smile as if he sensed my madness. Then, as Willy returned his attention to his magazine, I did notice his fidgety jaw muscle from clenching his molars. He was nervous too.

In Anchorage, I expected freezing temperatures, and yes, if I am honest, maybe a few igloos and Eskimos. After all, this was Alaska. But Anchorage looked like any big city, with towering high-rises downtown, and even, similar to Vancouver, snow-covered mountains in the background. It was as sunny and warm as our home that we had left just hours ago.

Early the next morning, I hurried Willy to the railway station, wanting to grab a good seat on one of the double-decked yellow dome rail cars that would take us to Fairbanks. As soon as the doors opened, I pushed and shoved—the way it was done in Switzerland—my way through the crowd on the platform and stormed up the stairs to the dome. Something felt different though—different because nobody pushed back. A few passengers even stepped aside to let us pass. It was simply amazing how relaxed everybody around us was, filing in, joking and laughing with each other as if they had been friends forever, finding spots, content with wherever they ended up sitting.

Willy sank into a red vinyl-padded bench, stretching his left leg into the aisle. I sat up straight and looked out the window from which we would enjoy a 360-degree view.

Thirty minutes into the ride, there were no more cities or villages. I had never seen so much land—surprisingly, uninhabited and mountainous. As the train rattled through Denali National Park, the Alaska Range stood to the west, Mt. McKinley towering proud and tall, as if daring climbers to make it to the snowy top—or not. Suddenly, our Swiss Alps seemed less unique.

The steel wheel's monotonous droning became voices—of my mother, father, sisters, brother, and girlfriend. I heard all their tearful good-byes before I walked through the passport control booth at the Zurich International Airport only six weeks ago. I heard my parents' half-hearted blessing, "You hardly know this man." And I felt another stab at my heart, remembering my beloved brother Kurt's hurtful accusation, "Don't do this, Verena. Don't walk out on your country and family. It's betrayal."

His words nagged at me still. I had never thought of it that way. What was so wrong following my heart, marrying the man I loved, even if it meant moving to a different country? True, my decision to do so came about rather quickly.

Six months after Willy and I had met, and carried on an uncomplicated long-distance relationship between our homes in the German-and French-speaking parts of Switzerland, he emigrated. It was November 22, 1977. Between then and my arrival on May 2, 1979, we saw each other three times. Three brief, all too short visits during a year-and-a-half.

I looked over at Willy who was with his big hands resting on his lap—these reassuring hands I fell in love with first—fast asleep.

Fairbanks. At three o'clock the following morning, sun rays streaming through the curtains of our hotel room woke us up. We tried to go back to sleep, but it was impossible; we were wired like kids on a sugar high. We dressed, ventured out and found a coffee shop that was open twenty-four hours.

Early still, we made our way to City Hall and the registrar's office, where we waited in front of the door until they opened. We applied for our marriage license and took the instructions for the blood test to get done at the walk-in clinic. With the formalities out of the way, we spent the rest of the day as tourists, and I was still on a quiet mission to find a dress.

By midmorning the sun stood noon-high, yet it wasn't warm enough to take off our coats. We strolled, among the few other sightseers, around Alaskaland, the pioneer theme park.

Inside a mesh-wire-fenced grassy area, we spotted a moose. While Willy retrieved his camera and bid me to pose in front of the enclosure for a snap shot, the colossal animal strolled calmly closer to the fence, so close that I heard it breathe behind me.

"Make it quick," I said getting uneasy.

"Done." Willy stepped toward the fence.

I grabbed Willy's hand and turned around. A droopy nose pocked high over our heads at the mesh-wire. Looking straight ahead, my eyes leveled at the animal's furry mass hanging from its chin.

"Wow," I said, "Everything in North America is huge."

We continued, sauntering on the wooden sidewalks, looking at the window displays: dream catchers, moccasins alongside sweat-shirts with kitschy animal logos. In one of the souvenir stores Willy pointed out a shiny package of chocolates called, "Moose droppings." It became clear to me that this tourist village was hardly the place to be looking for a wedding gown.

When we came to the Chena River, we decided to climb aboard the sternwheeler SS *Nenana* for a self-guided tour. As we sat on deck, on a white painted bench, the fresh air blowing at our faces, Willy patiently translated from a brochure. Captivated, I forgot my wardrobe concerns for a while.

For these early pioneers, who traveled the Tanana and Yukon Rivers in search of gold, their farewells to the families left behind in their old countries were final. The long and dangerous voyage overseas could cost them all their savings and for many, their health. But that was just the beginning. Once here, they marched, carrying with them their meager possessions into formidable territory in search of gold, riches, happiness, and prosperity. Many died young and poor.

Compared to us, these early settlers were heroes, and their journey, a life-altering decision—a one way to "no return".

The next day, June 7, 1979, was going to be our wedding day. We stopped in at the Fairbank Airport's tourist information center to ask for a street map of Barrow, but what we got was a lot more.

Willy and a young lady, who helped him, carried on a vivid conversation of which I only understood bits and pieces. The travel agent's face became more and more agitated, her forehead frowned. I picked up the word "booze."

Willy thanked her and we walked out.

"Booze?" I asked, "What's booze?"

Walking toward the check-in counter, my soon-to-be husband said, "She warned us not to fly to Barrow, unless we go on an organized tour. Booze is alcohol, and according to her, Eskimos, when they get their hands and throats on it, become violent. Last year, a tourist couple got shot."

"Shot?"

"Yep. Shot and killed." Willy who had already had time to digest all this, handed the tickets to the stewardess and continued lightly, "the good news is, there is a hotel and she thinks there is a church."

My mouth, all of a sudden, became very dry. *What were we getting ourselves into?*

"Don't panic," He reassured me with a forced chuckle, "Barrow is a dry town. It's illegal to sell or buy alcohol."

Obviously, not a foolproof system.

When we climbed the steps, entering the midsized Air Alaska plane and found two empty seats, Willy asked, "Are you scared?"

"No," I lied. "Are you?"

"Nah."

Willy rummaged in his backpack for the camera. I looked around. Only half the seats were occupied. Behind us slouched an unkempt-looking man with dark tanned skin. He was, I decided, boozed. Across from us sat a middle-aged man who, with his black rimmed spectacles, looked like a professor or a scientist. He spoke to me and I looked at Willy for help.

"Not for work," Willy answered for me, "to get married."

The man spoke again.

Putting the camera on his seat Willy translated, "He assumed we were flying to Barrow to work on the meteorological research station. Apparently, people flock to work up north for the money." Storing our luggage into the overhead compartment, Willy finished, "Then he asked if we knew what we were doing."

The boozed passenger behind us mumbled something.

"Pardon?" Willy said to him.

"It's not nice what the White man did," he repeated. Black eyes stared at us.

Before I could comprehend the words fully or analyze the strange look, the passenger beside us redirected my attention to him by saying, "Congratulations, I guess." He removed his spectacles and hung them on the pocket of the seat in front of him. He leaned back in his chair and closed his eyes.

We sat down and buckled up. Willy and I held each other's hands tight during takeoff.

"Don't worry," he said, "we'll be okay. I'm sure these people are not *that* bad."

"Maybe the tourists provoked them?" I speculated, but wasn't sure I believed it.

The land below became flat and we saw fewer and fewer trees.

"Welcome to the Arctic." The pilot's voice announced, "We have just crossed over the Arctic Circle."

Promptly, the stewardess handed out official parchment certificates. We rolled them up carefully. The offered sandwiches, however, Willy and I both declined.

Gradually, the barren land transformed into a leopard skin tapestry: vast grassy and mossy planes speckled with frozen lakes and streams. As the plane circled in descent, we spotted a ridge of ice along the shore of the Arctic Ocean. Beyond, there was a wide sapphire strip of open sea and then more ice.

BARROW

HOLDING ONTO EACH other and carrying our suitcases, we walked through the spring-soft dirt-roads of Barrow, searching for the hotel. Summer's receding snow was undressing the village. There were no trees. There were no roads, just mud, puddles and litter: pop cans, papers, bones—yes, bones and permanently parked four-wheelers with flat tires. A patchwork of metal sheets covered the roofs of paint-chipped, weathered homes. Some windows were covered with plastic.

The air was cold, but pure. Oddly enough, it didn't smell of garbage. If it smelled of anything, it smelled of ice, even though from where we walked, we could not see any. The streets seemed deserted, the scenery like that of an old, soundless black and white movie.

"Why don't they clean up this mess," I whispered to Willy.

By the time we reached the only inn, the Top of the World Hotel, my shoes were heavy clumps of mud. The unpretentious lobby was carpeted, the counter as shiny as in any four-star hotel. The staff, wearing clean blue and white uniforms, billed us royally for our bridal suite, but the room was not at all what I had seen in glossy magazines. Glancing out of the window, however, made everything luxurious. Down by the beach, a jagged mount of ice rose from the frozen ocean into an overcast sky. How could something so desolate be so beautiful?

Reinvigorated, we unpacked in a hurry and, with Willy's Swiss army knife in his pocket—just in case—we left the hotel to find a church and a pastor.

Outside we noticed a black pipe coming through the windowless side wall of the hotel and, supported on pillars about three feet off the ground, continuing toward the beach. We followed the contraption all the way to where it disappeared into the ice.

A cold wind made us pull down our toques and zip up our jackets as we climbed the frozen crest. From there we marveled at the open gap of water, the sapphire strip of ocean we had spotted from the airplane. Further out to the north, the prodigious ocean was frozen, rough, choppy, and intriguing, so very different from the frozen lakes at home. We looked west, south, and east. Except for the ice swells, Barrow and its surroundings, as far as our eyes could see, were as even and level and mountainless as I presumed the Canadian Prairies to be.

Breathing in the frigid, cold air was like drinking a shot of liquor—soothing liquid pouring down the windpipe, warming me from within. I leaned into Willy's tall chest, cherishing his protective embrace.

On our way back up the road, toward the village, we saw a dark figure step out of a house. We slowed our pace. I positioned myself partly behind Willy's back, hiding only enough so I could still observe.

The man, dressed in a brown jacket with its fur-trimmed hood framing his face, walked gingerly toward us.

"Hi," he said, as he passed us.

"Hello," we answered, looking at each other with relief, and then following him with our eyes.

I said, "He's nice."

"Very."

We proceeded along the "streets" of Barrow, strolled by the police station, the Brower's Café, two churches, and a Quonset building, which was the general store.

"Do you think this is the only store here?" I asked with a sinking feeling.

"It sure looks like it, doesn't it?" Willy said.

The few villagers we encountered wore the same wonderful parkas we had noticed on the first man. Most of them nodded in greeting or said hello. Their friendliness encouraged us to step into a residential area.

In front of a rickety fence lay sharply amputated huge fins. Next door, in the driveway, stood a pickup truck, its box loaded with bloody pieces of black-skinned carcass.

"Eww." Instinctively I wanted to crinkle my nose, but there was no rotting or foul odor at all. "Are those pieces of a whale?"

"Must be," Willy said. "Isn't that what they hunt?"

Within an hour, we had roamed most of the village and returned to a church that we had found not far from the hotel. When Willy knocked on the side door of *The Assembly of God,* I felt my heart beat faster.

A tall, big man with a white Santa Claus beard welcomed us into his office. The plywood walls trembled when he closed the door. He moved two wooden chairs in front of his large desk and gestured us to sit, then walked around it, plunked himself down into a squeaky, frayed armchair and looked at us with a wide grin on his face.

In a loud and clear voice, the man, I guessed him to be in his thirties, said, "I'm Pastor David Wilson." He talked differently than people from Anchorage or from Vancouver for that matter. It was not a British or any accent I recognized. His speech had a captivating twang. "Well, ma friends, what brings y'all into the house of the Lord?"

Willy explained our reason for coming to the "end of the world."

"Have either of you been married before?"

"No," answered Willy for both of us.

"Praise the Lord." His face beamed with pleasure as he pushed himself up from the chair. "Hey, man, hallelujah," he belted, raising his hands. Then, shoving them into his trouser pockets, clinking what was in there, loose change or keys, he asked, "How long are y'all in town?"

"Until tomorrow," Willy answered.

"Hey man!" He raised his voice even louder, looking up at the ceiling as if to make sure the good Lord heard him.

Again, there followed a conversation of which I could only guess the content. Finally, I understood, "Great. That's just wonderful."

Willy and the pastor shook hands. To me Willy said, "We're invited to a Bible study tonight and following that, Pastor will perform our ceremony." He embraced me and smiled, "We're getting married amongst Eskimos, isn't that exciting?"

Pastor Wilson cleared his throat to get in a word, "Do you have rings?"

"Actually . . ." Willy explained that we wanted to do what the Natives did when they got married.

Pastor David laughed so loud that the thin window rattled.

"What's he laughing at?" I whispered to Willy, who was listening to pastor's explanation.

"The pastor said," Willy imitated the intriguing accent, "The Natives here, ma friend, are called Inupiat and when they, like all Christians, exchange vows in church, praise the Lord, they also exchange rings."

When Willy inquired about a jewelry store in town, he found out that there was only a souvenir shop in the airport building.

Pastor Wilson concluded by my silence that I didn't understand much English. Next thing I knew, I stood in front of the big man, practicing the vows. "I, Verena Rechsteiner take thee . . ." The scrambled words that came out of my mouth didn't sound like my voice. My hands felt sweaty and my heart raced; I felt dizzy.

How would I know what I promised?

Kool-Aid and Caribou Stew

RELUCTANTLY, I PULLED the jean overalls from the suitcase. "Let's get married in these," Willy had said when we found them at Army & Navy in Vancouver. I believed that I was playing along with a joke and answered, "Sure, let's." Only, Willy had been serious and here we were now, in the Top of the World Hotel, getting dressed in overalls. *What will the pastor think when we show up wearing these? At least I'm going to get married in clean shoes.* I disappeared into the bathroom with my boots.

At the church, we were led into a bucolic side room without windows. Backless wooden benches stood along the walls. Willy and I huddled close together, leaned against the wood paneling, and watched Inupiats trickle in. Acknowledging us with nods, they found their seat while murmuring to each other in their native tongue, a medley of clicking sounds and guttural consonants coming from deep down their throats. The room smelled of damp wool.

"You look absolutely beautiful," Willy whispered into my ear.

"I do?" I said, but thought. "I do not feel beautiful. I look like a farmer's helper."

"Stunning," Willy affirmed, "Your eyes are especially blue today."

The pastor entered. I studied his face, but he showed neither shock nor surprise at our clothes. He introduced us to his wife Debbie and the modest congregation of about fifteen parishioners and went to the bench, where he pushed the button on a tape recorder.

"The recording," Willy whispered, "will be broadcasted later over the radio."

The Bible study started with a loud prayer. Other than that, I don't remember much of what followed. First of all, I didn't understand what was being said and secondly, the fish dinner we had eaten earlier lay heavily in my stomach. I took deep breaths, trying to stay calm. Standing up front, with his hands in his pockets, Pastor David rattled his coins. Every once in a while I understood, "Hey man. Praise the Lord, hallelujah." Was this a dialect thing, this "hey man" I wondered, but found it pretty cool, coming from a pastor. I studied the locals' dark round faces. Their black, wide-set eyes almost disappeared in the smooth skin when they smiled, but even without smiling, they looked happy and content.

The thought that in a few minutes, I would become a married woman stirred my nerves to the point of panic. Certainly, fear was written all over my face. I looked at Willy, who sat composed and confident, holding my right hand in his.

Suddenly, it was over. The pastor went to the door and people stood up and also left the room. I looked at Willy, who shrugged his shoulders.

My heart sank.

Not to have any friends and relatives present was tougher than I had envisioned. When planning this wedding trip, Willy and I had agreed not to invite any of my family, since his parents and brother could not make a journey like that. By not inviting family members, it didn't seem right to invite friends. Now to picture us all alone, getting married with only the pastor and his wife made me sad. Being at the end of the world to begin our lives together, lost its charm fast.

Like two forgotten sheep, we sat on the bench for what seemed an eternity, waiting for the pastor to come back. Then Debbie reentered, gave us an encouraging smile, sat behind the keyboard, and started to play softly. One by one, the church members came back in. Most of the women had changed into parkas made of vibrant-coloured fabric, some with exotic flower patterns, flowers they had most likely never seen nor smelled. It didn't make *me* feel any prettier. At that point, I became ashamed of my unworthy attire.

A middle-aged man carrying a mandolin and a woman, wearing a long gown in the deep blue colour of the Beaufort Sea, stepped in front of the keyboard.

Willy's hand dug into my palm, "Are you okay?"

I nodded, trying to control my emotions. These strangers, from whom we thought we needed a Swiss-army-knife-protection, cared enough to stay and witness our wedding, cared so much that they changed into their traditional costumes.

Pastor David said a few words. The couple standing by the keyboard bowed to us and then the lady nodded to her partner. He plucked the strings of his mandolin while she sang in clear, joyful soprano. The serenade made my skin tingle.

When they were done, Debbie placed her hands on the keyboard and started playing the wedding march. We didn't know what to do. It finally sunk in that my Dad was not going to give me away. I looked at Willy who again raised his shoulders, shaking his head.

"Please," Pastor invited us to step forward.

We rose and made the few steps toward the front.

Willy's palm was wet with sweat as he repeated the vows, loud and clear.

At my turn, I opened my mouth, ready to speak, but no sound came out. Pastor David repeated, very slowly, what I was to say. It took several attempts; finally, in a squeaky voice, I stuttered the vows.

We exchanged our souvenirs, Willy placing a silver and ivory ring on my finger and I pulling the bolo tie with a polar bear carved on ivory over his head.

"Ladies and gentlemen," the pastor said, "I present to you, Mr. and Mrs. Berger."

Everybody clapped and we kissed.

Pastor David introduced us to Noah and Molly Itta, two elders, who had agreed to be our witnesses. The old Inupiat couple didn't say much. But after signing the wedding certificate, I saw in their eyes, while they held on to our hands for just a bit longer than necessary, their sincere well wishes. I knew then I would savor that moment and forever remember the warmth of those soft, old hands.

Following the laughing crowd into the hallway, Willy put his arm around me. "We did it."

Inhaling deeply, I thought I smelled my mom's homemade beef casserole. Then I saw the buffet. One lady ushered us to join the line up to the paper-covered table with huge stainless steel pots on it. Willy and I each grabbed a white plastic bowl.

"Caribou stew," said the lady ahead of us pointing to the slow cooker with the steaming content.

I hesitantly retrieved the ladle half full, poured the stew into my bowl and grabbed a bun and a plastic spoon. Everybody ate while standing. The meat tasted so good, I went for seconds. Willy brought me a clear plastic cup with bright red liquid in it.

"Kool-Aid."

"Cool . . . what?"

"Kool-Aid."

"What's Coolaid?"

"It's like syrup. Just drink it. It's sweet."

Debbie tapped Willy on the shoulder, "Come," she said.

We followed her to the far end of the table where a rectangular slab of cake with blue icing sat. Written in white icing sugar was: "Congratulations Willy and Verena." *How did she do all this in one afternoon? What a truly amazing woman.* I so wanted to tell her how much I appreciated all that she had done for us, but the best I could do with my nonvocabulary was to give her a big hug and say, "Thank you vary vary vary much."

Everybody gathered in a half circle around us.

"You have to cut the first piece and feed it to your wife," Debbie demanded.

People cheered when Willy pushed it into my mouth.

Then, one by one, the citizens of Barrow embraced us. Someone presented us with a Bible and opened the cover to the first page, where people had signed their names and written words of advice: "Be happy." "Make lots of children." "Love each other forever." "May God bless you and keep you forever and always."

It was fitting that we didn't have fancy diamonds to exchange. No worldly goods could match this experience and the sincerity we felt from our new friends.

When we finally parted from the pastor and his lovely wife, it was after midnight. Outside, children ran, playing catch as if it was the middle of the day.

Willy said, "Debbie told me the sun won't set until August now."

"And in the winter? How long is it dark?" I wondered.

We could only guess.

"I can't believe Pastor David wouldn't take any money from us," I said.

"I tried. He refused." Willy put his arm around me. "Care to dance Mrs. Berger?"

We waltzed through the soft ground in the direction of the hotel.

When Willy carried me across the threshold, the state of my shoes was not important anymore.

The next morning we walked through the village again, only this time without the Swiss-army-knife. The wind blew in our faces and through our layers of clothes.

I pointed at a pile of plastic bags and pop cans beside a precariously leaning fence, "It would look so much better if . . ."

"Are you the kids who got married yesterday?" A woman said, stepping out of her modest home. She stretched out her hand to congratulate us. "My sister Bertha was at your wedding last night."

All the way to the Brower's Café, more people talked to us. It seemed every citizen of Barrow had a relative who attended our wedding. We had become celebrities overnight.

Inside the coffee shop, the teenaged waitress also came to our table with an outstretched hand, "I'm Dora, Molly and Itta's granddaughter. I wish I had a real wedding present," she said and handed us a paper place mat that she had signed like a wedding card. "Good luck to you both."

As we ate the crispy bacon, soft eggs, and golden brown fried potatoes, Willy asked her about the "meat" we had seen lying on the pickup truck.

"Whaling season just ended," she explained. "Each catch is cut up and shared amongst the villagers." The young server gave Willy time to translate for me and then continued. "The feathered fins we have no use for, except for a few that we polish, etch, and sell to tourists."

Since we were the only customers, she felt invited to sit at our table. "Whaling is a big part of our livelihood," she continued. "Now, some environmentalists want to take that away from us too."

Again, Willy repeated in Swiss German.

"Ask her about that research station," I said. "Didn't that bring jobs?"

Dora got up from her chair, "Yes, but for whom?"

Leaving those words pondering for a while, she seemed to get lost in thought. Then, she continued, "The 'progress'" she said, signaling quotation marks with her fingers around the word progress, "that we have been given is impossible to dispose off." She grabbed the coffee pot from behind the counter. "Three feet into the ground, everything stays frozen in summer and winter." Topping our cups and then sitting back down, her face became serious, "Working in this diner, I hear a lot. I hear tourists' prejudice remarks about the way we live."

Understanding—when Willy finished retelling—the connection to the comment of the Inupiat in the plane two days earlier, I felt myself blush.

Blush for "what White men did" and blush for my own judgmental thoughts.

Why I am Canadian

I GREW UP IN a picture-perfect country, where every citizen owns a savings account. After completing a two-year apprenticeship required to qualify as sales clerk in a stationery store, I presumed it might be interesting to work in a shoe store.

The owner laughed at me. "What do you know about leather and fine shoemaking? Please, you are not properly trained."

Obviously, the shoe store was out of reach. I decided to leave the German-speaking area and move half-way across Switzerland, one hundred kilometers west, to the French-speaking area. The chance to meet new people and learn about a new culture excited me. But my enthusiasm was dampened with my first customer entering the stationery store.

"Bonjour, Madame, est-ce que je peux vous aider?" (Good morning, madame, can I help you?)

"Oui, vous pouvez m'aider. Allez chercher quelqe-un qui parle propre français." (Yes, you can help me. You can go and find a person who speaks proper French.)

Stunned, I went and asked the manager to help me out. She explained to the customer that I was indeed a qualified sales clerk. The customer let me help her without trying to hide her annoyance.

This scenario repeated itself many more times. I was a stranger in my own country, left with two choices. Either go home or quickly learn to speak French without an accent.

Two years later, I handed in my three-month's notice to which I endured a severe reprimand for leaving after such a short period of employment.

Then, I followed my boyfriend to Canada, the country of space and tolerance. My knowledge of English consisted of: "Please," "Thank you" and "I do not understand."

That summer, the workers at the *Vancouver Sun* were on strike. Striking was a new and foreign concept to me. It left me with no other choice but to march along busy Broadway Street in Vancouver, British Columbia, and enter every store in search of a job.

With my little speech written on a piece of paper, I read, "Hello. My name is Verena. I loock for vork."

Although I could not understand the answers, the tones of voices, and the shaking of heads indicated that there was no job for me. Finally, on the fifth day, I hesitantly walked into a McDonald's restaurant and recited to a young woman dressed in a reddish-brown uniform: "Hello. My name is Verena. I loock for vork."

"Just a minute," the clerk said and left.

I waited. A man came toward me, smiled, and invited me to sit on one of the stiff chairs.

"Hi, I'm John. How are you?" he said.

"I am Verena. I loock for vork."

"So I see."

He handed me a form to fill out. It was not hard. "Name," "address," and "phone number,"—I could understand without my dictionary.

"Can you work full time?" The man asked.

"Full time?"

"Can you work all day?" He explained.

"Yes, I vork every day." I said.

He wrote on the application: "Hired."

A new word.

The next day, I started my job as a hostess. I had to empty the garbage cans, clear and wipe the tables, and ask customers if everything was satisfactory. In the beginning, I eyed the customers, waited until they were busy chewing their food, then quickly asked them, "you like?" and left before they could swallow and answer something I didn't understand.

Soon, I learned many new words and two weeks into my new job, I was promoted to server and French-fries girl. Eventually, I was asked to do the opening shift in the morning.

After work, after showering off the grease at home, I ventured downtown in search of stationery stores. My language skills had improved so that I could properly ask for the manager at Williams and Mackie on Pender Street. He didn't need anybody.

"Go back next Thursday," Willy encouraged me.

The following Thursday he still didn't need anybody.

"You must go back next Thursday," said Willy.

The Thursday after that, I came home with the same disappointing answer.

"Next Thursday, go back again," Willy insisted. "Show him how badly you want that job."

That week, I got hired. But I panicked because I was to start within four days.

Feeling guilty for walking out on McDonald's after just six weeks and without having time to resign in writing, I was rather shy to hand in my notice. To my surprise, the manager shook my hand and congratulated me on finding a better-paid job so soon.

With my notebook and pen in hand, I walked the aisles of Williams and Mackie, writing down the names of the articles that I knew so well, but could not name. A smartly dressed businessman entered the store.

Eagerly approaching the customer, practically cutting him off, I greeted him the way I had learned at McDonald's: "Hello, may I help you?"

"Yes," he smiled. "I need paper clips."

I knew "paper" but "clips" didn't sound familiar, so I simply asked the customer: "What are paper klips?"

He smiled broadly and reached for my hand. "I will show you." He led me to a shelf and said, "These are paper clips. See? Next time, you will remember, eh?"

"Yes. I will. Thank you."

Making our way to the cash register, he asked me where I was from and if I liked it in Vancouver. He told me my accent was charming and paid for his purchase.

"Welcome to Canada," he said and left.

This scenario repeated itself many times.

I was home.

Broadcasted on *CBC First Person Singular*

Canadian Dream

TRAFFIC LESSENED considerably, once we drove north on Highway 99, out of Vancouver. Soon, instead of smelling gasoline fumes, we inhaled the rich scent of ocean and forests. The Sea to Sky highway wound between steep hills from where luxurious mansions clung onto cliffs' edges, whereas on the opposite side of the road there were dramatic drops, allowing a magnificent view onto Horseshoe Bay.

The VW bus, as most people know, does not have an extended hood, which put us very close to the action on the road. Some curves were tight-angled—the road's shoulder uncomfortably narrow. However, this was nothing compared to the driving conditions that would await us.

This weekend excursion into the Cariboo, British Columbia's interior, was our virgin voyage with our canary yellow 1974 VW bus. During the past six weeks we had worked hard, cutting fabric, sewing pillows, sawing two-by-fours, hammering together bed and cupboard, and installing propane lines, all of it without a sewing machine or power tools. We did all of this while working in the city's July heat and the back alley's dust, where our van was parked. Our open-air garage came with the basement suite we rented near Main Street. To get away from the perpetually damp and bug-infested studio for a few days was no punishment.

Willy maneuvered past Whistler without turning into the village. The resort, similar to Davos in Switzerland, noble enough to host royalty, burned holes too deep into pockets of folks like us. On an old 8-track, the Chipmunks harmonized in their animated voices. We sang along, "Time for you . . . and time to cheer . . ." and decided right then, our bus's name would be Alvin.

In Pemberton, a small town surrounded by flat, lush farmland, we stopped for dinner and then continued east. The pavement turned into gravel and the road narrowed.

Hans, Willy's coworker at Freybe Sausages and fellow Swiss immigrant, had warned us, "Don't drive the back route, unless you have a four-wheel drive vehicle." But Willy was confident, our bus would prove roadworthy. Leaving the climb for the next morning, we searched for a level spot at the foot of Mount Currie and parked for the night.

After our dinner of cold cuts and bread, we inaugurated the propane stove by heating water for coffee. Then, we converted the seating arrangement into a bedroom. Our camping equipment worked flawless, everything was hunky-dory until Willy went to the "outhouse."

He stepped outside, leaving the sliding door open. Before he disappeared behind a cluster of willow trees, dozens of mosquitoes came buzzing in. I slid the door shut. Not a minute later, I heard Willy yelling, "Open that door. Hurry. Open that door!"

His pants still half down, he stumbled into the van.

It took us a couple of hours to finally squash and kill the last annoying insect inside the bus.

We woke early, hoping a before-dawn start into the woods and mountains would reward us with a bear sighting. And also, we were anxious to get to Williams Lake where Hans was going to show us his land.

He bragged about buying the property to everybody who would listen. He had a right to boast though because back in Switzerland, owning land was simply unthinkable, particularly for young citizens like us. In a country smaller than Vancouver Island, and inhabited by 7.5 million people, buying land was as unattainable as climbing the Eiger North Wall wearing sandals. Yet here in Canada, Hans had done it.

Alvin climbed and climbed, slower and slower. Deciduous trees became scarce, evergreen forest more dense. The temperature dropped. The gravel road turned into a soft dirt trail. Willy navigated around rocks and roots.

Several times the front wheels lost traction on the wet, slippery path. I held onto the door handle with mounting anxiety.

Our car radio had lost contact long back, and we hadn't seen another vehicle since last night. I wasn't so sure that I wanted to see a bear anymore. Just when I was contemplating about admitting my fear and suggesting turning back, we came around another bend, spotting a meadow with a few rustic homesteads. On a dead tree trunk hung a sign, "The Murdock's" and underneath it said, "B&B."

"Wow, Look at that. Someone actually lives here?" I asked, relieved that we were no longer the only humans far and wide.

"Sure looks that way, doesn't it?" Willy said. "This must be D'Arcy."

I thought I detected some relief in his voice as well. But our ease was brought to an abrupt halt only minutes later, when, back in the woods, Willy slammed on the breaks, coming to a stop inches from a pool of water covering our track.

"I better check it out," he said, sliding from his seat.

Willy picked up a stick and stuck it into the puddle to measure its depth. "Now what?" I asked.

Throwing the stick back, he said, "I say, pedal to the metal." With an earnest face, he climbed back into the driver's seat, held on to the steering wheel with both hands and accelerated, "Let's go."

The van jumped, and so did we. Willy hit his head on the ceiling. I screamed. The bus scraped its underbelly but came out on the other side.

We cheered, high-fiving each other.

"We just baptized Alvin." Willy laughed.

We continued, driving beside gurgling creeks and then meandering between deep, velvet-looking forested valleys to one side of the road and razor-sharp cliffs, threatening like growling watch dogs on the other. In the far distance, snow-covered peaks reached into the cloudless sky. There was no village, no gas station, no restaurant—only nature.

Finally I understood. I understood that people could actually get lost. Last year, before I immigrated, Willy wrote to me about hikers and hunters going missing in the Canadian forests. For me it was incomprehensible. Why couldn't one simply search for the light between the underbrush-free trees and walk to the end of a grove? Looking around now, I got it.

Anderson Lake came into view. We stopped and got out. The pure cobalt blue of the glacier water took our breath away. The air smelled of snow. My teeth clattered from the cold wind, and we quickly found refuge inside Alvin's cockpit again.

For the next three hours, the winding road didn't seem to end. Eventually, though, we descended along Seton Lake, into Lillooet, where we filled gas, removed our jackets, and bought coffees in Styrofoam cups and a bag of potato chips.

"What a great time saver this eating and drinking while driving is," I said, looking out the window, admiring the changing scenery while fidgeting on my seat to relieve my mosquito bites' burning itch.

"How can you stand it?" I asked Willy

"The itching? Don't scratch."

That, I found, was easier said than done.

We now traveled on a more open, dusty gravel road. The beige hills cluttered with tea-green bunch-grass was my idea of the wild west. In Canada, I realized, not only people are multicultural and versatile, so is the landscape. To our left stretched a dangerously steep and deep canyon. We noticed patches of green, irrigated fields and soon thereafter, came to a hamlet with weathered looking houses.

"Dog Creek." Willy said, "It's a reserve."

"Reserve?"

"Indian reserve. Indians own this land. We can't call them Indians though. They're natives."

"Why?" The heat stifled me; I opened the window.

"I don't know why, really. Indian has become a forbidden word."

"Remember Karl May's *Cowboy and Indian* stories? My brother used to read them to me." I reflected back to our childhood games. "Remember Winnetou, the Indian chief . . ."

"And Old Shatterhand," Willy finished for me. "Wasn't Old Shatterhand, a German immigrant?"

"Yes." I said. "He came to America and found the Indians, ehm, sorry, the natives. My brother and I used to act out warrior scenes, pretending to ride horses chasing each other, and later smoking the peace pipe around a bonfire."

For a while, we drove in silence, Willy munching chips and I looking for natives and tepees. I spotted a few playing children and was disappointed that they were normally dressed, didn't even wear feathers in their hair.

The air smelled of sage. I coughed from dust being blown into the car and wound up the window. Hundreds of cows and calves grazed on immense fields. I searched for the barns.

"Where do these animals sleep at night?"

"They sleep outside."

"And where do they sleep in the winter?"

"Outside," Willy answered.

I shook my head. Back home, a farm consists of a few acres of land and maybe a dozen cows. The herd is brought into the stable every night.

By the time we entered Williams Lake via Dog Creek road, it was dark. City lights reflected on the black lake like a still firework display. We parked the van on a side street and went to sleep.

The next morning, Willy kicked off thick layers of dried up mud behind the tires. Black specks of dust (which we learned later was fly ash) covered the windshield and roof of our van. Alvin needed a bath.

It was hot and sunny as we drove through town. With thick smoke rising from cone-shaped chimneys, Williams Lake looked less romantic in the daytime. I noticed a different kind of traffic than in Vancouver. The vehicles here were mostly pickup trucks, some new and shiny with big tires, others rusty and dusty, and a few so banged up that I was afraid they'd start dropping parts on the road.

From 150 Mile House, we drove east onto Horsefly road. Following Hans' instructions, we turned, half an hour later, onto a mud-dried driveway. On either side of it stood rugged fir trees in the lush underbrush. We came around a curve, and a wide and rocky field opened up. It stretched far into the sky. The sky! I had never seen such a vibrant azure sky.

Then, ahead of us, I spotted Hans. Balancing a few pieces of lumber on his shoulder, he was walking toward the very beginning of a structure. He must have heard the motor of our bus as he turned around, promptly dropped the wood and waved unabashed. Our friend wore a cowboy hat, running shoes, and a pair of underwear.

Getting out of the van, I tried not to look at his crotch. "Beautiful!" I said.

Hans straightened his back and opened his arms. "Eighty acres," said the proud landowner, standing there, still in his white briefs.

"Do you know how much this would cost in Switzerland?"

"Sure do," he laughed, finally grabbing his jeans. "Anybody here can buy land," he said as he pulled up the pants.

"Well, well, well!" came the voice from the now open Boler door. Ursula stepped out of the baby blue camper that was parked next to the wooden frame structure. "Look who showed up!"

"Since you spend all your weekends up here now," Willy said, "we thought, we better come and check this out."

We declined the invitation for coffee being way too excited to sit down. Instead we let Hans and Ursula show us around. After inspecting the future barn, we walked across their huge, rocky meadow.

"How did you find this place?" I asked.

"As you know, we've traveled all over the world," Hans said. "This area, situated between the Rocky and Coastal Mountains, is one of the safest places on earth to live."

"How come?" I inhaled deeply the aroma of ripe grass.

"The Fraser River flows deep in the valley, too deep to flood. And the Interior Plateau is too narrow for hurricanes to build. Besides," he went on while bending down and picking up a fist-sized rock, "we're at an altitude where we will enjoy four seasons. Our land will feed off the snowmelt." Reaching a barbed-wire fence, Hans threw the rock over it and then leaned onto one of the fence post, "We plan to run a sheep farm here."

"Aren't you a butcher like Willy?" I asked while discretely scratching at my mosquito bites. "I didn't know you were a certified farmer as well."

"This is not Switzerland." Hans got serious. "This is Canada. And we're living the Canadian dream."

Ursula stood, nodding to everything her husband said.

"Even though it is 1979, we can live free like hippies. No permits required for buildings, farming, or cutting trees." After a pause he added, "Not yet anyways."

"Are you telling us?" I asked pointing to a tree over by the house, "You can cut that tree," and, pointing to another down the driveway, "and this tree" and waving my arms, "and all those trees? Are you seriously telling us, without joking, you can chop all of these trees if you want, without a permit?" And then I couldn't resist finishing, "in your underwear?"

"Butt naked if I want to," Hans beamed, "and so can you." Then he added, "Scratching makes it worse."

HAPPY DAYS

EVEN THOUGH SHE was a doe, we named the goat Fonz because of her impeccably groomed appearance and because we knew "happy days" had just begun for us.

In the feisty early March wind of the Cariboo, we cleared our newly purchased rural ten-acre property—a parcel of land from a recently developed subdivision along a new road named Paradise Drive—with chain saw and wheel barrow to construct a road and pull in a mobile home. As soon as the ground softened, we planted our first garden and built a rickety log fence around it.

The well-meant advice of our neighbors, "Build a solid fence before you get the animals," fell on deaf ears and the how-to books they brought us got stacked away. Anxious to start our hobby farm, we adopted our first animals and by April 1981, our little menagerie included a puppy named April, a couple of cats, and a beautiful Nubian goat—Fonz.

Quickly Fonz became our buddy. With her chiming Swiss bell around her neck, she followed us wherever we went on the property. She nipped at us with her nose to get our attention and loved playing catch. Fonz must have deemed to be a person and—had we let her—would have come into the house and probably crawled into our beds. She complained loudly when we tied her to a tree at night.

During the following weekends we laboriously pounded treated posts into the rocky ground with a sledge hammer. Then we doctored our blistered hands and massaged each other's sore backs. We ignored our neighbor's "Told you so."

Instead we redesigned the fence-line so that we could use a few poplar trees in lieu of posts. We pulled second-hand, sagging barbed wires between the posts and trees and proudly introduced Fonz to her new habitat.

Every night, we put her inside the fenced area. Every morning she greeted us outside our front door. Every weekend we fixed the fence; after all, where there is a will, there is a way. But *Homo sapiens* aren't the only species with a will.

One day in July, when we returned from work in town, I headed, as always, directly into the kitchen and checked on my slow-cooker supper while Willy stayed outside and fed the animals.

A few minutes later, he came stomping in, "The garden's gone!"

"Haha, you're funny," I laughed. "I told Cathy that since she just moved in and her garden won't be ready until next year, she could come and help herself to our lettuce."

"You don't understand." My husband took my hand and led me outside. "The garden is *gone!*"

A hurricane. A hurricane must have swept through the garden. But beside the disaster area stood Fonz with, I swear, a smile on her face. It was she, our own goat, who had banqueted on our organic food supply.

In my hysteria, I grabbed the next best twig and ran after her, all the while verbally abusing her. Fonz thought we were playing catch. With her long ears flopping, she jumped a few steps, stopped, turned around, and looked at me as if asking, "Coming?" The Swiss bell around her neck sang to her dance. Just when I thought I could hold on to her tail, she slipped away again—and again.

To our ad in the local newspaper, we received a phone call from a young mother who was interested in purchasing a goat. She was hoping that her son, who was allergic to cow's milk, would tolerate goat's milk. I did tell her that our goat was easily spooked and that we might have a little difficulty loading Fonz onto her pickup truck, but that she was welcome to come and meet our pet.

When the truck stopped in front of our house, the goat stood at a safe distance. Mom and toddler got out. The four-year-old and Fonz made eye contact and slowly walked toward each other. As the child stretched out his short arms, Fonz bent down and gently licked his hands. Mom opened the tailgate and, without hesitation, the goat jumped in.

One year later, a little wiser and our barbed wire fence two strings higher, we dared another attempt. Willy bought a snow-white Saanen goat. He decided to call her Celine, after his aunt Celine who supposedly had the same kind of beard.

For Celine, it was as big a challenge to escape as it was for us to keep her fenced in. According to the teasing counsel of our neighbor, we removed the Swiss bell that we had lovingly passed on from Fonz and replaced the leather collar with a rope and a two-by-four pendant. Every few days the piece of wood was exchanged with a bigger one until one day Celine and her piece of lumber were too awkward to jump the fence and the board around her neck too bulky to squeeze through the barbed wires. We bathed in the glory of success for two months.

Then a cougar jumped the fence and ate Celine.

Maybe goats weren't our forte. Maybe we needed to think bigger.

The following year, we decided to expand our home operation and invested our savings in twelve piglets. Piglets, however, are quite a bit smaller than goats. The rules that apply to goats, don't apply to piglets. Twenty-four sides of bacon mysteriously walked off our property.

We never found the hole through which the piglets had escaped and—noisily and hungrily—returned four stressful (for us) days later. But we were finally ready to read the books on hobby farming and fence building that our neighbors had brought us three years earlier.

First published in *Country Magazine*

EARL OF SWITZERLAND

W HEN HE FINALLY saw me, he was close enough to hug.

"Grandpa," I wrapped my arms around his big chest. "So good to see you. How was the first flight of your life? Did you find a customs officer who spoke German?"

Loosening my grip, Grandpa said, "Pas de problem."

"Grandpa, we speak English here, not French."

Instead of acknowledging my comment, he looked around the crowd of passengers and greeters. Then, as if recognizing an old friend, he smiled at a middle-aged man and lifted his tweed cap in greeting.

The man nodded, "I see you found your granddaughter." He padded Grandpa jovially on the shoulder. "Nice to have met you, Earl. Enjoy your holiday eh?"

Earl? I must have misunderstood. Grandpa's name was Jacob. "Besides," I thought, "Grandpa doesn't speak English, how could these two have communicated?" I reached for the suitcase. "We better get going, Grandpa. Remember I wrote to you that we would still have a long way to go."

Favouring his left leg, he picked up my pace. "Is it really six hundred kilometers from Vancouver to Williams Lake?" he asked, stopped and pulled his cigar case from his inside jacket pocket. "And we're driving all that today?" He lit his cigar, "That's insane."

In Europe, when driving that many miles, you cross at least two countries. Nobody does that in one day. It didn't matter, though, because Grandpa dozed off before we left Richmond, didn't even stir when I removed the burning cigar from between his lips.

My grandfather was our first family visitor since we immigrated. How would he like the Cariboo and—more importantly—what stories would he tell once he returned to Switzerland?

It rained when we arrived, seven hours later, on Paradise Drive. I maneuvered our VW bus station wagon along the side of the muddy driveway, so the wheels could grab onto grass and roots. Coming around the last curve, I honked the horn.

Willy appeared from the woodshed. "Welcome to our home!" He helped Grandpa out of the car. "You're going to love it here."

We showed our guest our mobile home and his small bedroom. He nodded with approval. We showed him around the yard and introduced him to our first construction, the outhouse. He was less impressed.

"No running water at all?"

"Not yet." Willy explained, "But Jacob,"—Willy called him by his first name—, "this is our land. We own ten acres." Opening his arms—the same way Hans had shown off his land to us only a few months earlier—Willy continued, "The trees, the garden, the wild flowers, and the worms beneath the earth, they're ours."

"Do the worms know that?" Grandpa asked, tiptoeing clumsily with his bad hip, trying not to sink into the soft mud with his dress shoes, back to the house.

"Willy and I thought it would be like the good old days for you."

"My dear sweet child, this is 1981. I'm eighty-one years old. I have no desire to relive any old times let alone the ones without utilities."

After unpacking his suitcase he lit a fresh *Roessli Stumpen*, went to the boot-room, brushed the dirt off his shoes and smeared black polish on them. The smell of smoke and turpentine awakened childhood memories of Grandpa's shoe repair shop. *Of course he is particular about his footwear.* I made a mental note to find a pair of rubber boots for him.

Turning the shiny shoes in his hand, Grandpa said, "Things will be better once your driveway is paved."

I bit my lip. On our list of things to do, paving our driveway was number never.

Willy had taken holidays, thinking Grandpa would enjoy helping him around the yard. But with every board Willy hammered onto the new addition, Jacob, handing him the nails, said, "I don't wanna tell you what to do, but don't you need a building permit for that? This is not the way I'd do it."

Watching Willy pour cement for a rain water holding tank, Jacob, removing the cigar from his mouth, said, "I don't wanna tell you what to do, but will this be inspected? I bet it's going to leak."

Leaning on his shovel while Willy dug in the dark earth to secure the pig's trough, Jacob said, "I don't wanna tell you what to do, but are you allowed to keep farm animals on this property?"

Even though it rained every day for the first week, Grandpa refused to wear the rubber boots. When he went to the outhouse he said, "Things will be better once you have running water." When he came back into the house, he brushed his shoes and said, "Things will be better once the driveway is paved."

Ten days into Grandpa's visit, the veins on Willy's neck threatened to explode. Hoping a change of scenery might cheer Grandpa up, we decided to take him to a rodeo.

He didn't bite. "Oh that's just movie stuff. It's not real anyway."

"I'll show you how real it is," Willy promised. "Let's go."

Willy dug out all his charm and wits to persuade Grandpa that our second vehicle, Vera the rusty truck with the missing tailgate was roadworthy, before he slid onto the middle of the vinyl-torn bench. We followed in, banged the doors shut and pulled out of the driveway.

"Stop the car," Grandpa yelled. "We can't go."

"Now what?"

"Your rear view mirror is cracked."

"Jacob," Willy said, "this is the Cariboo. We have a license. The engine starts. The stirring wheel works. Believe me, we're good to go."

Grandpa shook his head. "Tsk tsk tsk."

In Switzerland, a truck like ours would have failed the mandatory inspection long before we had bought it for three hundred dollars at the forestry auction the previous year.

Willy drove through Williams Lake, showing off Boitanio Mall shopping center, our train station, the stationery store where I worked, and the almost completed Provincial Resource Building.

"We call this building the sardine can," Willy explained pointing to the oval structure, "obviously because of its architecture."

Pointing to the building beside it, I proudly said, "That's where Willy was sworn in as Canadian citizen."

"When was that?" Granpa asked.

"A couple months ago," Willy said.

"You don't remember the exact date you became Canadian?"

"Isn't that something?" Willy said, surprised at himself. "But I do know the date of arrival. November 22, 1977."

"May 3, 1979." I threw in.

Finally, Willy chauffeured around the brand new Sam Ketcham recreational center and swimming pool before turning back onto highway twenty, heading west. We left first the stampede grounds and then the stocked-up timber yards and smoking beehives behind us.

Grandpa looked out the side window. "Why did you decide to live in such a dusty town?"

Nothing is good enough. Suppressing a sigh, I proceeded to tell my grandfather how we had fallen in love with the Cariboo and the idea that we could afford to buy land. Even though, we purchased our ten-acre lot before we traveled across Canada, before driving through the marvelous flat Prairies, visiting Ottawa and the Parliament Building, before strolling through the romantic streets in Quebec City, meeting the warm-hearted people of the Maritimes, and before seeing floating ice bergs off the east coast in Newfoundland, we never found a place more suitable for us.

"We love the snowy winters here," Willy said, driving over the Sheep Creek Bridge. He slowed to a crawl for us to enjoy the spectacular view of the Fraser River and then accelerated for the climb. Minutes later, we arrived on a plateau.

"This is the Chilcotin," Willy said.

Grandpa straightened. "Look at the size of these farm fields."

Without turning his head off the road, Willy said, "They're cattle ranches with hundreds of animals, Jacob."

"Grandpa, these cows don't have stables," I said before he could ask and added, "they stay outside during summer and winter."

"Unbelievable," Grandpa shook his head.

When the road led us along a forested area, Grandpa said, "Somebody should clean up this underbrush. It looks so messy."

"Jacob," Willy laughed, "where would 'somebody' start? Have you seen the sizes of Canadian forests?"

"Have a cigar," I changed the subject. "Relax and have a smoke." I worried more and more about what he would tell our families back home.

At Riske Creek, Willy decelerated, turned off the road and parked on a grassy field where a bunch of trucks, trailers, people, and horses had gathered.

The people we walked by, mostly natives of the Chilcotin, Tsilhqot'in, nodded hello and offered friendly smiles. Some held beer bottles in their hands; one man walked unsteadily.

Seeing the harsh looking bleachers we were going to sit on, I regretted not having packed blankets. We found an unoccupied bench and sat down. The dry, dusty ground in front of the fence was littered with empty pop cans and discarded paper. I gave Willy a worried look, but Grandpa didn't seem to notice any imperfection.

With a burning cigar in his mouth, he got up from his seat and made his way down to the rodeo ground. With every horse that bucked, every cowboy who rode, he got closer to the log fence where some men had climbed onto. Grandpa leaned against the untreated logs and watched. One cowboy had his arm in a cast. Still, he mounted a wild horse. People howled and clapped wildly. So did Grandpa.

We alternated from watching the rodeo to watching Grandpa, who by now stood on the bottom log of the fence. Every once in a while he was gesticulating with the spectator beside him. All afternoon, my grandfather didn't move from his perch.

We literally had to pull him, covered in dust because he was so close to the action, away. The man beside him yelled after us, "Nice to meet you Earl."

"Earl?" I said it aloud this time. "He called you Earl?"

"That's my name."

"Grandpa, your name is Jacob."

"I looked it up in the lexicon before I came. My name is Earl," he insisted.

On the tip of my tongue was, "You can't translate names". But I didn't want to argue. At eighty-one years, I reasoned, Grandpa was allowed some leverages and calling himself Earl could be one of them. Instead I said, "Grandpa, I never knew you liked horses so much."

During the drive home, we listened. We really listened for the first time, and found out something new about my grandfather.

While serving in the Swiss army, Grandpa was a wachtmeister and in charge of installing telephone connections to watchtowers, fire and command stations. With a beaming face, Grandpa described how he was given a horse to supervise the progress at the different locations more effectively. Then his face changed into a frown, "It was not always glamorous and fun. During the hard years, (meaning WWII) the rain and mud were the worst. I cleaned my horses' hoofs for hours, scraping out small stones and dirt. Animals and soldiers, we were wet for days and days."

The more Grandpa shared, the quieter Willy and I became.

Alas, the next day, no longer desperately trying to impress my grandfather, I called our neighbor, asked if we could come over and take a look at his logging crew.

"This is Jacob," I introduced Grandpa when we arrived, "Unfortunately, he doesn't speak any English."

John stretched out his hand, "Nice to meet you."

With hilarious facial expressions and waving arms, the two moseyed over toward the horse pasture, forgetting I was even there.

Grandpa stayed for lunch.

The following morning early, John phoned, "Where's Earl?"

"Earl?" I laughed, "My Grandpa's name is Jacob."

Done with this nonsense, I went and asked my grandfather, "Show me where you found your name in the dictionary."

And he did. His full name was Jacob Graf. Grandpa introduced himself like a proper Swiss does, with his formal, his last name and Graf translates to Earl.

Earl visited John and his horses every day. Because Earl didn't have time to polish shoes anymore, he wore the rubber boots his new buddy had lent him. Smoking his evening cigar, Earl enlightened us on the gentle procedure of horse logging.

"How do you know all this?"

"John explained it to me," he answered as if I had asked a rhetorical question. "Next time when I come, I must stay longer."

A few weeks after Grandpa's return to Switzerland, we apprehensively opened letters from home. My brother wrote, "Grandpa is driving everybody crazy with his Canadian stories." My sister's letter read, "All we hear from Grandpa is: You should immigrate to Canada; you should see how they do things over there." My mother wrote, "Grandpa said you are living his dream."

Grandpa, alias Earl, did not visit us again, but for many years, floods of relatives and friends, friends of relatives and friends of friends, and people we never saw before, did.

I think of Grandpa often, especially when it rains. Sometimes I feel his spirit so much, I can almost smell cigar smoke and shoe polish.

GONE FISHING

OUR VW BUS fought up that slippery slope like a salmon on his last run. Most winter days we needed several attempts to make it up Paradise Drive, but the winter of 1981 and 1982 was particularly snowy, cold, and icy.

At the bottom corner, the junction of Desautel Road and Paradise Drive, new owners had recently moved in and it seemed that we had become their evening entertainment. As soon as our car started spinning, this redhead showed up at his living room window, making funny faces at us, laughing his head off.

The day our van slipped into the ditch we learned that our new neighbor was not a mean man. After having his fun, he disappeared from the window and moments later, came out the door.

"Hey man, I'm Patrick. I'll pull ya out."

Patrick's rusty pickup truck coughed like a tired tractor, but it did manage to get us back on the road.

"See ya tomorrow," he laughed. Before turning to go back inside, he invited us to his home for a drink on Friday night after work.

That's when we met his wife Debbie, baby son, toddler daughter, golden lab, Whiskey and the rest of the neighborhood. In the small living room, people sat on chairs, the couch, and on the floor, drinking beer and chatting. A half a dozen children squeezed behind the sofa, eating chips and drinking pop.

It had been two-and-a-half years since we immigrated but life was still a perpetual English-as-a-second-language class room for us and that day we learned about ice fishing. Patrick showed photos of his catch the previous weekend. He was so proud that his hair took on a darker shade of copper. The picture showed him bundled in heavy jacket and toque, standing beside a hole in the iced-up Dougan Lake, grinning widely. His fingers were deep inside a fish's throat.

"Weren't you cold?" I asked.

"I'm Irish. I don't get cold."

When Willy and I left for home that night, we noticed eerie red clouds in the sky and ran back to tell everybody there was a fire nearby. The only positive thing about the ridicule we had to endure for panicking over Northern Lights was that nobody got burnt—physically.

Fridays became TGIF (Thank God It's Friday) nights at Patrick and Debbie's. One evening in January—the temperature had dropped and stayed at more than 30 °C below zero—we listened intently as our new friends talked about their electric block heaters for their cars (unheard of in Switzerland) and heating tape that can be wrapped around water pipes to prevent them from freezing. Willy and I exchanged looks but kept quiet about the melted snow we had been drinking for the last three days.

Another Friday, Patrick handed around a cigarette to share. To the man sitting beside me he said, "Don't give the joint to the hillbillies; they don't smoke weed."

"What's weed?" I whispered to Willy. "And why are they sharing a cigarette?"

"Can't you smell it?" he whispered back.

I didn't smell anything. I didn't know about joints and weed. What I knew—or at the time thought I knew—was, the neighbors called us "hillbillies" because we lived on top of the hill and because they kept asking if Willy's name stood for Bill.

During the hockey play-offs, when there happened to be a game played on Friday, the television was turned on. Even though we had heard in Switzerland about "The Great One" number 99, Wayne Gretzky, we didn't realize how important hockey is to Canadians. And we didn't know, that here, the sport is played with sticks *and* fists. When the Edmonton Oilers played against the Vancouver Canucks, the hooting and hollering, I was sure, could be heard all the thirty miles into town.

When I brought tea to drink one Friday night in April, the neighbors guessed correctly that I was pregnant. The very next morning, Debbie drove up to our home. Leaving her old truck idling, she walked to our front door carrying a heap of clothes over her arm. I invited her in.

"I can't stay," Debbie said. "If I turn the engine off, the truck won't start up again. Here," she handed the clothes, "we're done having babies."

Taken aback by her generosity I asked, "Are you sure?"

"Absolutely positive," Debbie smiled. "Last week, Pat had a vasectomy."

My dictionary confirmed why Patrick had walked around his yard as if he had peed in his pants. What puzzled me, though, was their charitableness considering how they struggled, living from paycheck to paycheck.

Debbie and Patrick were always broke and their truck always needed repairs. Whenever Pat had a chance to work overtime at the copper mine in McLeese Lake, he did. On payday—or at the latest, the day after his night shift ended—he and his wife hired a babysitter and went on the most elaborate date available in Williams Lake, dinner, and a movie. They returned from town with toys for the kids or a new fishing rod for Patrick and then, they were back at being broke and a rusty truck still needing repairs.

Two months after receiving the clothes, I learned how resilient the Irish really are. Debbie came to reclaim the maternity wear.

Our pregnancies bonded us. Over the summer weekends, if Patrick didn't go fishing, our husbands helped each other build additions to our homes while we women alternated with the cooking. Debbie taught me to can fruit and I shared our garden harvest, which consisted of carrots and cabbage. Everything else froze, half-ripe, during a full-moon night in August.

My garden was still more profitable than Debbie's patch, which she used as a pig pen. Sausage (that was the sow's name) was to loosen the ground for planting next year.

The day Sausage escaped through the fence, we all happened to be sitting in the backyard, ready for the last barbeque of the season. Pat shot up from his lawn chair. "She's heading for my crop," he yelled, chasing, with Whiskey in tow, after the pig into the bush. There must have been an important crop behind the poplar trees for back and forth they all ran, Pat, Whiskey, and the pig, the pig screeching, Whiskey barking and Pat using language I had never heard before and—am not sure I should repeat. Witnessing Patrick's temper flare, I finally understood why people called him "redneck."

Once Sausage was back in the pen, Pat calmed down as fast as he had exploded. His face and neck back to their normal colour, a beer in one hand and flipping the trout on the grill with the other, he said to Willy,

"You oughta come fishing sometime. I could borrow my Dad's camper, take it an' a case o'beer to Bella Coola. We'll catch us a heck of a salmon or two."

"The only fishing I do is at Safeway," Willy said.

"I'll come fishing with you," I offered.

At that, Patrick guffawed. "That ain't gonna happen. Ever." He roared so much, his body doubled over. "At fishing time, sweet girl, the're no broads . . . ehm . . . women allowed." He had a hard time controlling his laughter but added, "Even if you weren't so close to poppin' your baby."

For a week now, my suitcase stood packed in the corner of our bedroom. I was feeling anxious. My belly had dropped and the baby moved more frequently.

It was the last day of September at nine o'clock when, suddenly, the power went out. During thunderstorms, this was not such an unusual occurrence, only the weather that day had been sunny. We decided to call it an early night and Willy lit our way to the bedroom with a candle.

A few hours later, I nudged him, "I think my water broke."

Even though, the contractions were still twenty minutes apart, we decided to pack up and head out. The drive to the hospital would take us forty-five minutes.

When we saw candles burning through the living room window in the house at the bottom of the hill, we parked the VW and got out. Debbie met us at the door, grabbed my shoulders hard, and pulled me as close as she could with both our bulges.

"Verena," she said in a shaky voice. "You go and have your baby. But I must tell you, tonight, on his way home from his day-shift, Pat died in a car crash."

Willy had to help me back to the van. We drove in stunned silence. On our way to Williams Lake, we passed the accident scene and saw the mangled truck wrapped around a hydro pool.

Oliver Patrick Berger was born by caesarean section twenty hours later. I signed myself out of the hospital to attend the funeral. During the ceremony, held in the backyard, we learned that Patrick had been epileptic. While driving, he had suffered a seizure, losing control of his body and the steering wheel. The truck raced full speed into the ditch where it banged brutally against a hydro pool.

Standing by the grave, feeling weak and faint, I read the plaque: "Gone fishing."

THREE STEPS FORWARD
AND TWO STEPS BACK

B ESIDES WILLY'S FULL time job at the slaughter house in town, he supplemented our income freelance butchering. One Saturday, after a pancake breakfast with our one-year-old baby, Oliver, he drove off in our Honda station wagon to slaughter two cows in Horsefly.

In a few hours, he would return with a bucket full of blood-and-shit stained coveralls and fifty dollars in cash. On a good day, there might be scraps, leftovers customers didn't want to eat like: tongue, heart, or tail. And if Willy got lucky, the farmer would let him keep the hide. Its price fluctuated with the commodity market and sometimes sold for as much as twenty dollars.

Oliver and I had spent the day roaming around our property, picking rose hip berries.

I was rinsing them at the kitchen sink when I heard the roar of a motor getting louder. Shaking the water off my hands, I called Oliver and together we went to greet Willy. He waved a fifty-dollar bill in one hand and carried the soiled clothes bucket with the other. Inhaling the irony smell of cold blood, I grabbed for the pail and the money as we kissed.

Willy turned to his son. "Hello, sunshine," he said taking Oliver's hand, "Come, help Daddy unload."

What he retrieved from the trunk was not what I expected. No leftovers. No hide. A hairy hind quarter, hip to hoof.

"What the heck?" At the same time I said it, I noticed the broken front light.

"Surprise." Willy said, giving me a lopsided smirk and a shoulder shrug. "That deer," he sighed, "came out of nowhere, standing frozen, on the road staring into my windshield."

The rest of the story, or at least the beginning of it, we had heard from many others living in the Cariboo. Willy tried to avoid the animal, but struck it nevertheless. Injured, it limped into the wood. Instead of driving away though, Willy stopped the Honda on the road's shoulder. Not wanting the deer to suffer, he grabbed his knife and followed the bloody tracks. Not far into the bush, the deer had collapsed and died. Willy made a quick decision to take what he could and with a few skilled cuts, amputated a hind quarter.

"Isn't that illegal?"

"Only if you get caught," Willy reasoned. "The piece I took will feed us for a good while."

The deer parts and the rose hips were the only profit we made that day, for the deductible on the car insurance was fifty dollars. This was not the only time when, despite hard efforts, our only reward was a bite to eat or—experience.

There was the year we decided to keep one half of the pigs we raised, butchered and sold in the backyard, for ourselves. The thought of placing "real" meat, rather than offcuts or cooked organs on the table, made my mouth water.

Getting ready to bring the hind piece for the ham to our friend Hans, who had a smoke house, I loaded toddler Oliver and snacks in the car. The snacks were for me, I was pregnant again, and hungry was my middle name.

"Did you load the ham?" Willy asked.

"No, it's on the counter in the boot-room."

"No, it's not."

Willy and I looked at each other for about two seconds and then we yelled in unison, "Max" and ran to find our German shepherd. We found the dog, but not the meat. Had I not been impaired by my belly, I would have been tempted to give Max a spanking. On second thought, though, our dog was not to blame. Max must have assumed his find was just an especially juicy treat Willy had brought home from his job at the slaughter house in town.

The loss of the ham threw me into a crying frenzy for two days. Willy blamed that on my out-of-sorts hormones. Eventually I got over it and life went on—until the next crisis.

There was the year when we, in the true spirit of nepotism, hired a neighbor to drill our well. Substituting the solid rock for casing, we paid a very reasonable amount for the three-hundred feet of drilling. For almost a year we pumped fresh spring water out of that well. With our two little helpers, Oliver and his younger sister Melanie, we nurtured and grew a lucrative vegetable and flower garden. Then the water became sandy, the lever became harder and harder to push down and eventually nothing more could be pumped out. The verdict: our well had collapsed.

We paid our neighbor a visit. Over a tense cup of coffee session, we first sternly demanded fresh drilling, then soberly requested new casings, then quietly asked for some sort of other fixing. In the end, Willy stooped to begging for at least some monetary compensation.

"Sorry folks, there's nothing I can do for you," he said lightly. "What can I say?" He laughed, "I went belly up. Would you like a refill on that Java?"

This setback was more than two steps. This was returning to the beginning, collecting rain water for a long while, and taking on any extra job we could find in order to eventually pay for new drilling.

Anon, there was the job we accepted from a customer who needed his pig slaughtered.

Whether Willy butchered our animals or someone else's, the kids and I stepped inside the house until the shooting was over. As soon as the pigs hung on the steel frame and hooks, "Hansel" and "Gretel" and "Porky" and "Snorky" became meat. Willy took pride and pleasure in showing his toddlers how to open a gut and remove the organs. He let Oliver and Melanie feel the still warm heart and liver.

That day, I stayed inside even after the killing was done, keeping an eye on the apple pie in the oven and making coffee. Once the skinning and quartering were done and the meat loaded back on the truck, accounts would be settled at the kitchen table.

Shoveling pieces of my warm pie into his mouth, Willy's customer revealed that he had no money to pay us. He could offer us his two geese as trade. "They're great watch dogs," he cackled, while chewing with an open mouth.

We already had a watch dog. What we didn't have was a pond.

"You clip their wings and they won't fly away," he reassured us.

Left between the choices of two birds or nothing, we settled on the poultry. The poor, penniless man got up and shook Willy's hand to seal the deal. I watched him drive down our road. A bad feeling festered in my gut, the doubt that we would never see him again, or meet his geese.

Contrary to my expectations, he brought the white feathered creatures promptly the next day. We didn't have the heart to clip their wings and butchering them was a taboo topic after twenty-four hours. They became great playing excitement for Oliver and Melanie and the talk of the neighborhood. Named after Wilhelm Busch's children's story of two young prankster boys "Max" and "Moritz," they made an unbelievable racket, quacking as if the world was ending every time someone approached the house.

Then one morning into the third week, they were gone.

My suspicion was, the geese were trained to fly back home. Who knows how many other bargains had been made?

None of the setbacks left permanent scars. Even though, the words thrifty and frugal were no metaphors, the years we lived up on the hill on Paradise Drive rewarded us with the most heartwarming memories. Memories we still reminisce and laugh about at every family gathering.

1986

OUR BUSIEST VISITOR year was during the summer of 1986, when Vancouver hosted the World Exposition on Transportation and Communication. On May 2, we watched on TV, with Canadian pride, Prince Charles and Princess Diana officially inaugurating Vancouver's hundredth anniversary celebrations, Expo '86.

Early in July, my parents flew into Williams Lake and relaxed with us here in the Cariboo for ten days. Then, I drove them, with our toddlers, to Vancouver. For three nights, we stayed at one of the many, specifically established for Expo '86, B&Bs. Every morning we boarded the new, fabulously fast-moving Sky Train in Burnaby and within less than half an hour exited at the Water Front Station. Vancouver showed itself in the best light; the sun was out. From the impressive Canada Place, Canada's pavilion, with its roof built with five distinctive sails, we looked across Burrard Inlet to North Vancouver and Grouse Mountain.

A special shuttle-train transported us from Waterfront to Stadium Station on the north shore of False Creek. The Plaza of Nations was bustling with tourists, street vendors, guitarists, singers, jugglers, and oodles of volunteers, who were easily recognizable by their bright-coloured T-shirts and even brighter smiles. Here and there we stopped and tasted a bite of grilled burgers, spit-roasted pork, and deep-fried doughnuts.

My father learned patience during those few days, standing in line for hours, being "herded like cows," as he put it, between rope-connected posts, to get into the Swiss and other countries' exhibitions.

After I dropped my parents off at the airport, I went home to get ready for the next thrust of guests, my sister Anita and her brand-new husband, Markus.

They flew in less than a week later, but started their holiday in Vancouver, enjoying the hustle and bustle of Expo '86 on their own before driving up to the interior.

While my sister and handsome brother-in-law were repacking to continue their honeymoon, paddling the world-famous Bowron Lake Canoe Circuit, Willy's mom, Muetti, and her brother, Fritz, also arrived.

Our little house was bursting at the seams. Every bed was occupied; hence, the kids camped on the carpet. We almost had to set up a numbering system to use the only washroom. We had built two benches and a wooden table for the patio especially so that we could all sit together for meals. Uncle Fritz, always outside with a burning cigarette between his yellow-stained fingers, helped Willy, along with Markus, with the chores. Anita and Muetti assisted generously in the kitchen.

Over a pork roast dinner, Markus egged Willy and me on, "You should come to Bowron Lake and canoe the circuit with us."

"Yeah, right." I laughed. "Dream on."

"We can babysit," offered Uncle Fritz. While lighting a new cigarette with his old stump, he looked at Muetti, expecting her enthusiastic support.

"Ja ja." She smiled bravely. "We can look after Oliver and Melanie."

"Yeah! Hurray!" cheered the kids.

I was unsure what exhilarated them more, spending a week with Grandma and Great-uncle, or without us. Willy and I felt the same way about having a week to ourselves but didn't admit it quite so openly. Since Oliver and Melanie were born, our time alone was rare. We didn't have extra money for babysitters. Nor did we have family backup readily available. Extravagances such as vacation a deux were nonissues.

"Hmm . . ." said Willy, "a week's holiday."

"It's not just the children who need taking care of, you know." I said, waving away his musing. "Pigs, rabbits, cats, dogs, and the vegetable garden need looking after."

Uncle Fritz got up from his chair.

Watching him disappear down the hall, I said, "Someone has to collect the food-scraps from town. It's a two-hour round-trip." All the while I was speaking, my mind was going through the closet in search of camping clothes.

For Uncle Fritz too, it was a done deal. The chain-smoker and retired Swiss military medical instructor returned with his first aid kit.

"I never leave my apartment without this," he said, unlatching the hinges and lifting the metal lid. "Here." He retrieved sample-sized portions of suntan lotion, bug repellent, and blister cream, "take those with you. You want to be prepared."

Anita, giving me a sisterly shove, said, "I guess you're coming."

Willy was voted responsible for the menus and food-rations. Taking in account an experienced outdoor man's council of bringing treats, he went a little overboard. He packed two bottles of red wine, a glass jar of pickles, frozen steaks, fresh bananas. A couple of books in case one of us felt like reading.

The next day, at the Bowron Lake Circuit registration center, when my sister and I, with the assistance of our husbands, got strapped into our backpacks, the loads were so heavy that we could not rise from the bench. Quickly, Willy and Markus reorganized, each accepting more of our weight in their own packs.

We trudged the first 2.4 kilometers on narrow paths through dense forest until we came to Kibbee Creek, where we all dropped our backpacks by the shore. Willy and Markus got ready to return and fetch the canoes.

"Markus," I said still breathing heavily, "why don't you drop your load around your neck?"

"Are you kidding," he said, caressing his bulky video camera, his binoculars, and his Kodak, "leave all this here and miss the chance to film a bear or moose?"

He turned to catch up with Willy who had started marching back, yelling to us, "I'm never letting go of my equipment."

Standing there alone in the wilderness, surrounded by tall evergreens and thick underbrush, we heard, besides the sound of the rippling creek and buzzing mosquitoes, all kinds of strange noises coming from the woods.

"What are we going to do if a bear shows up?" Anita asked.

I whispered, "We don't even have a bear spray."

To keep ourselves busy, we dug out the mosquito repellant and slathered ourselves thickly with it, both of us probably hoping it would keep more than just insects away. Then, holding hands, we stepped away from the backpacks—the food. Half laughing and half crying we waited for our husbands to return.

We heard crashing and cursing long before the inverted canoes' orange bows appeared between the trees. Willy and Markus, weak from the load, had lowered their arms so that their heads were inside the hull of the upside-down canoes. Two sets of legs and torsos approached wobbling. We watched Markus's right leg step off the path. He slid and slumped into the ditch, the canoe collapsing right on top of him. Markus's blaspheming drowned hollow from underneath the boat.

We sisters put our hands on our mouths, stifling our laughter, while Willy dropped his canoe and rushed to aid his tripped comrade.

With great difficulty, we got boats and loads and ourselves in the water. Willy and I, never having sat in a canoe before, realized his paddle stroke was so much stronger than mine. We zigzagged left and right but made no headway. Willy kept instructing me over and over on how to paddle properly, but I didn't seem to grasp the mechanics or produce the needed strength.

Finally, Willy said, "Why don't you stop splashing the water and fish instead?"

I embraced that excellent idea and brought out the rented rod, trying to figure out how to release the line into the lake.

The wind picked up, and it started to rain. By the time we reached the other shore of Kibbee Lake—our first camping spot and the beginning of the first portage—we were drenched. If it hadn't been for Markus's fire-starting expertise, we might have eaten steak tartar that night. It was a miserable evening, and we crawled into our wet and muddy tents early.

"What were we thinking?" Willy whispered, doctoring his blistered hands. "This is no holiday. This is more work than staying home."

"I'm cold and wet," I whined, disappointed at my own sissiness, feeling out of my element.

The following morning, over burnt toast and coffee, we decided to alternate with the cooking, to give each couple every other day "off." In the afternoon, while paddling side by side on Indian Point Lake, the clouds broke up and the rain stopped. The sun came out, and two loons swam and dove around us. Our good moods returned.

Willy paddled, I fished with, as told by the rental shop owner, heavy lead weight attached to the end of my line.

From the other canoe, I heard Anita point out, "Darling, look at Verena. She's taking another break."

Markus had no music in his ears for breaks. "Stop babbling, Darling. Keep paddling."

The following shore's transfer from canoe to trail didn't go over smoothly for my sister. Stepping out of her boat, Anita's right foot sank into a slough up to her knee, while the foot of her other leg was caught on the canoe's rim. Panicking, trying desperately and precariously to keep some kind of balance, she screamed, "*Darling!* I'm sinking!"

Instead of helping his new wife, whose legs seemed to spread apart more and more with her one foot sinking deeper and deeper into the marsh, Markus reached for the camera hanging around his neck and started clicking, infuriating my sister to the point of delirium. I might have run to help, but I was, once again, doubling over with laughter.

Willy—bless him—rushed to Anita and pulled her, minus one running shoe, from the bog. While the newlyweds bickered with each other like Archie Bunker and Edith, shouting profanities and "Darling" in the same sentence, Willy and I, holding our heads down to hide our grinning faces, searched for the sunken footwear.

The portage to Isaac Lake was fairly easy, and the next day passed without great theatrical interludes, since I'm not mentioning the little tiff Willy and I had, when the mundane water fight turned nasty. I called him the worst words ever said between us until then—and since—and the last words spoken between us that day, "You're a f-bleep—bleep." Like I said, a minor fall out not worth mentioning.

The weather, after the first rainy day, was uncharacteristically warm for the end of August. The jagged, snow-peaked Cariboo Mountains formed a scenic background to the valley. Thanks to Markus's persistent binocular-scanning, we spotted a black bear with two cubs, watched an otter at work, snuck toward and paddled very close to a moose standing on Isaac Lake's shallow shore, and watched eagles circling above us.

The five most challenging kilometers were paddling down the winding Cariboo River. We managed to maneuver our vessels between rocks, floating tree-trunks and branches, and came out without losing any gear or getting too soaked. On that stretch of water, I smelled fish and was confident to have success with my rod soon.

On Lenezi Lake, as before, Willy paddled, I angled, Anita complained, and Markus commanded her to keep moving. Sitting in the front of their canoe, she didn't notice that her rowing-partner had slacked off, launched his fishing-gear too and, giving his attention to his rod, was using his paddle only for navigating.

"I've got one!" I squealed. Jumping up, I almost tipped the canoe. Still screaming, I found my balance and started to reel against a strong pull. I didn't know I had this in me, this hunter instinct, not feeling sympathy for a second for the trout—or whatever fish it was—fighting to get off my hook. I reeled and released, and reeled more. Just as I leaned to drop my net, Markus yelled from his canoe, "*Got one.*"

Anita turned around. "*Darling!*" she yelled. I could hear in her voice disgust that he had fished instead of paddled, but also detected the joy underneath, the pride for his catch.

That night, we set up camp in a clearing by Sandy Lake and grilled our fish. The smell of burning wood and cooking fresh fish was the most blissful aroma I had ever inhaled. Never have I tasted such a succulent meal or eaten with more contentment. It was the perfect time for Willy to retrieve the last bottle of red wine.

Not just I, but all of us were in high spirits that evening and we decided to enjoy the sandy beach for a day of rest and keep our tents up for an extra night.

Willy and I were more than happy to prolong our second honeymoon, as we called this trip. This week in the company of my sister and husband without phones or any kind of radio contact, seven days without children, chores, and jobs had become days of sheer bliss.

Reinvigorated and refreshed, we tackled the last two lakes, Unna and Bowron Lake, returned our rentals, and drove home.

Oliver and Melanie were ecstatic to see us. Uncle Fritz was in a state of panic. One of the pigs had inexplicably dropped dead. Luckily, before we had left for Bowron Lakes, Willy had given our butcher-friend Hans' phone number to Uncle Fritz. He did call and Hans came and exchanged the carcass for three crates of crabapples.

Once Willy's uncle realized how nonchalantly we took the loss, he started beaming, "Look at the work I did," he said, pointing to our front yard with his left arm while bringing his cigarette to his mouth with the right hand.

Our property was transformed.

Uncle Fritz had raked together, piled up and burnt all detached underbrush, broken twigs, and grass. Muetti told us he had had several fires—naturally with water-filled buckets placed nearby—going all at once, spending his days outside, trailed by Oliver, from dawn to dusk. Proof of her words was the tin cans, half-filled with crushed cigarette butts on our patio, by the pig trough, the rabbit cages, and on top of the garden fence posts.

In the boot-room, I saw Muetti's week's accomplishment—dozens of jars of preserves.

"With my assistant," she boasted, holding Melanie by her hand. "This little one knew exactly where you keep your sugar and your canning supplies." She looked down at Melanie, "A real little mother hen this one is."

I was not surprised to learn that our three-year-old daughter had demanded a spot at the stove and, standing on her stool, had stirred the jam.

A day later, we piled into our Honda and drove my sister and her husband to the Williams Lake airport, then immediately with Muetti and Uncle Fritz to Vancouver. Once more we toured the Expo grounds. Four days later, before boarding their return flight to Switzerland, Uncle Fritz promised to come back and clean up the rest of our ten-acre property.

"I've never in my life had so much freedom to do what I wanted, when I wanted," he said. "You guys don't know how lucky you are."

His words made me reflect during our drive back to Williams Lake. Having lived in both countries, we did know how lucky we were. We did know about the old country's apartments' limited space and building-regulations' suffocating rules. Our children, on the other hand, took their freedom for granted.

Finally alone at home again—my other sister, Maegi, wasn't due to arrive until the end of September—we sat on the patio with Oliver and Melanie. One of our cats came in, carrying a kitten in her mouth. She dropped it at Willy's feet and left. Moments later she came back with another one, and then another one. Willy followed her and found a cardboard box, nicely lined with leftover carpet, placed in our woodpile—*Uncle Fritz!*

We found not one, but two such boxes. Our feline population rose to an all-time high of sixteen that summer of 1986. The cats and the left-behind medical box were the last tangible memories of Uncle Fritz.

Lung cancer claimed him before he could return.

Different Countries, Different Customs

FROM THE DAY Oliver first saw a school bus on the road, he couldn't wait to start kindergarten. School, as it turned out, was as much a learning experience for us as it was for our children.

On the early September morning, Melanie, our dog, Max, and I walked Oliver to the junction of Spokin Lake Road. We watched as the little tyke stretched his legs to climb the high steps into the yellow bus, grabbed a seat and grinned at us through the window. Melanie and I waved until the bus disappeared around the corner. Then, we headed back. By 8:30 a.m., our almost five-year-old daughter, our dog, and I were home again, having marched four kilometers. Melanie was ready for her first snack and I for another coffee.

In the afternoon, we repeated the exercise and waited anxiously for the bus. With sparkling eyes, Oliver summarized his day, described his pretty teacher, telling us all about his new friends—in English.

I asked, in German, "What did you say, Oliver? I can't understand you."

German, Swiss German, was the language we spoke at home and we intended to keep it that way.

On the third day, Oliver experienced his first bullying incident. Apparently, other children had made fun of his handkerchief. I took this personally.

My hometown, St. Gallen, Switzerland was and still is known for its embroidery and fine fabrics. My father, who was personnel manager in a handkerchief factory, used to supply us with tons of laced, stitched, and/or initialed hankies in every dye. I learned to care for them from my grandmother, washing the pieces of fabric, ironing them by carefully pushing the tip of the hot iron into the edges, and finally folding them so the ornamentations were visible on the top right-hand corner.

Stuffing a colour coordinated hanky into his little trouser pockets before trotting off to kindergarten was the dot over the "i," the icing on the cake, and my proud moment of perfection for the day. Thus, the following morning's whining, "I hate my handkerchiefs," fell on deaf ears. So I assumed, did my lecture to Oliver about feeling privileged and proud to own cotton handkerchiefs.

Since I am not a monster, I prepared, as consolation and encouragement, a prosciutto sandwich for Oliver's lunch. The salt-cured, paper-thin sliced cold-cut was a European specialty meat that I loved dearly, but bought rarely because of its high price.

In the afternoon, during our walk home from the bus stop, Oliver told me, between sobs, that nobody that day had wanted to trade his sandwich.

I was more than a little cross. "Why on earth would you want to trade your super yummy sandwich?"

"I wanted peanut butter and jam," Oliver explained.

From that day on, Oliver made his own lunch. We added items such as bologna-with-macaroni sausage meats, white soft bread, cheddar cheese, and peanut butter to our shopping list. The hanky ceremony prevailed.

By late November, it was pitch black when we left to accompany Oliver to the school bus in the morning. As soon as there was enough snow, Max pulled the kids on our wooden toboggan. When the temperature dropped even further below zero, the waiting students huddled in a circle by the bus stop, giving up the warmest, middle spot to the youngest.

More and more, Oliver talked English. When he got tired of my asking in German what he had said, he turned to Melanie who didn't mind what language she was spoken to as long as her playmate was back.

Melanie, we felt, was very mature for her age. Our strong-willed little girl had already once packed a plastic bag with socks and toothbrush and stomped out of the house, leaving "forever" as she had put it. And while other children emptied kitchen cupboards playing with pot and pans, our Melanie probed through the shelves rearranging pots and lids and lining up cans like soldiers on a drill. She knew how to boil tea. She "read" Snow White. Clearly, Melanie was ready for kindergarten.

With my gifted child in tow, I went to Oliver's classroom one afternoon, intending to ask his teacher where we can have children tested for early enrollment. After Ms. Bains' students were dismissed, the classroom left with only desks, toys, and the smell of crayons and cold lunches, we placed Melanie with a few blocks on the carpet. The teacher and I sat on mini chairs around a little table close by.

"You can't," she answered my request. "We go strictly by age. Melanie has to wait."

"But she is so ready," I argued. "And her birthday is in January and that will make her almost six by the time she can start."

"Sorry, Mrs. Berger. That is just the way it is here."

"In Switzerland . . ." I stopped myself from finishing. "Thank you for your time," I said, getting up.

Disappointed I called Melanie, "Come Sweety."

She hesitated to stand up and when she did, she left a dark stain on the carpet. I felt my face turn beet red.

"Don't you worry, Mrs. Berger," Ms. Bains said, "this happens all the time."

I bet it does. I bet anxious mothers come every day, telling teachers how mature their children, who pee on the floor, are.

When I accompanied Oliver to his first day of grade one at the beginning of September, I was more nervous than he. The kids stormed into the class room and claimed a desk while we mothers lined up along the back wall. Many pupils turned their heads, some with tears in their eyes, but I couldn't will Oliver to look at me.

Earlier, we had purchased all the items on the list of school supplies, including a box of Kleenex!

The classroom looked very colourful. Shelves with books and brightly labeled plastic containers lined the side wall. Behind us, posters hung from floorboard to ceiling. Even the two doors were plastered with notices. I listened with full concentration to Mrs. Meddaugh welcoming her new students and parents. Together, she told us, we could make this a great year.

"Please, parents feel free to drop in anytime. And if you are able to volunteer, you can contact me so that we can set up a schedule. I am grateful for any help."

I laughed out loud, then, realizing I was the only one, put my hand on my mouth, looking at everybody else staring at me. Wasn't this a joke? What does she mean, "help", "volunteer?" Parents are not qualified to teach. Isn't she capable of handling a classroom full of students? And if so, why on earth would she admit to it?

The teacher's incompetence was confirmed when I looked over Oliver's homework. First of all, the eight and a half by eleven sheets of paper looked like they had been through the first two of a cow's four stomachs. Secondly, even *I* grasped that the spelling was full of mistakes. Yet at the bottom left corner were stickers and tick-marks and words like "well done." I flattened Oliver's homework as best I could and stuck it inside a plastic folder.

The next day, Oliver brought me a note. In it the teacher requested that Oliver not have plastic folders as the other students didn't have them either. I sent a note back asking for a meeting.

"In regards to spelling," Mrs. Meddaugh explained looking over the incriminating sheet of my son's essay, "we focus first on writing neatly and on the lines. Later we will concentrate on grammar."

"No wonder," I thought, "what we were taught in nine years in the old country, children here need twelve years to learn." For me that was the last straw and I signed up as a volunteer at the 150 Mile Elementary School.

Walking down the shoes-and-jackets littered hallway, I noticed most classroom doors were left open. When I got to Oliver's class, I expected quiet little people sitting with straight backs and concentrated faces, each at their desks, working away. What I found was a zoo.

A cluster of kids crouched on the floor in a corner, counting marbles or something; a few students sat in a circle reading aloud and about five pupils, planted in the front row, were listening to the teacher while she was writing on her blackboard.

When Mrs. Meddaugh turned and saw me, she didn't flush in embarrassment of her unruly classroom situation. No. Calmly placing her white chalk on the ledge of the blackboard, she smiled and waved me over.

"I'm glad you came."

"Me too," I said.

I was given a book and a student and was told to sit in the last free corner for a private reading tutorial.

Suddenly, I felt overwhelmed and insecure. Could I do this? I, who still mispronounced so much. Two huge brown eyes looked at me expectantly.

"Well," I said to the cutie. "You're learning to read and I am learning to teach. Let's see if we can help each other."

Little Bruce didn't seem to question my credentials. Tears welled in my eyes with pride when I helped him sound out the word "cat." I forgot the commotion around me and didn't even hear the bell ring.

My weekly volunteering at school became my favourite days. I learned that reading in Canada is hugely encouraged. Instead of pounding information into students' growing brains for them to recite by heart, children here are taught how to find answers in books. Students are encouraged to have an opinion. School is not so much a military-style disciplinary environment; it's a happy place. And I had to admit, children do learn. Oliver matured into an excellent speller. Fascinated with sharks and dinosaurs, he read endless books on the subject. For each volume read, he earned cheers, stickers, and prizes. In fact, reading in Canadian schools is so big, each schoolhouse has its own library.

I don't remember stepping into a library as a child. In Switzerland, there were no libraries in school buildings. We must have had a town library, but I can't even recall where it was situated and I don't remember ever being inside it. (I understand things have changed in Switzerland since then and many school do have libraries now.)

Steady communication between teachers and parents was new to me as well. I enjoyed the photocopied notices that I regularly found in Oliver's lunch box. We were advised of upcoming sports events or excursions and cougar or bear sightings near bus stops. We even received an information sheet about a basic sex and molestation class that we had to sign if we agreed for our children to participate in.

In early May of 1987, Oliver brought a yellow piece of paper home, announcing that all the classes of the 150 Mile Elementary School would stand honor guard along Highway 97 when Rick Hansen rolled by on his last stretch of his "Man in Motion Tour."

During his forty thousand kilometer journey across four continents, Rick not only brought awareness about the difficulties people bound to wheelchairs face in everyday life, but he also raised millions of dollars for spinal cord research. Extensive festivities were planned for the wheelchair athlete's homecoming in Vancouver, where he lived. But Rick went to high school in Williams Lake, and we regarded him as one of our own.

Everybody in our community wanted to do something for our hero who had turned tragedy into triumph. (As a teenager, he had fallen from the box of a rolling pickup truck and landed in a ditch from where he would never get up and walk again.) Banners were hung; people lined the main street through Williams Lake. At the Stampede ground, we heard later, a packed audience waved yellow ribbons and balloons. Afterward many ran along as he pushed himself out of town.

The ascend by Sugar Cane Indian Reserve is steep, but a man who wore out ninety-four gloves and had labored his wheelchair on the Wall of China certainly could make it up the 150 Mile House hill.

As soon as Rick came into view, students and teachers, parents with toddlers, ranchers, and construction workers, started clapping and cheering. Melanie and I waived in front of Marshall's general store. Rick Hansen came closer and closer; he slowed down and steered his wheelchair toward the crowd. He stopped in front of us, stretched out his hand to me. Profoundly moved, any words I wanted to say stayed stuck in my throat.

The whole experience left me in awe. Not only for what Rick Hansen did, but for how we honored him; how our school district organized time off for students to celebrate a role model.

When Melanie finally was old enough to enter school, she too kept returning home with forms—forms to give consent for extracurricular activities. Thanks to their teachers' dedication our kids tried team sports, participated in athletics, signed up for debating classes, played musical instruments, and raised funds for school trips.

Willy and I finally learned that we needed to stop comparing what is incomparable. Immigration status had been offered to us by Canada. Integrating was up to us. With this new and improved attitude, we sailed through the remainder of our children's elementary school years.

FREE FOR THE PICKING

I SMELL THEM BEFORE I see them. The fresh, tantalizing fragrance of the most delicate of all wild flowers, the wild rose, puts a smile on my face every spring.

Down in Vancouver, cherry blossoms have come and gone. But here in the Cariboo, the last patch of snow melts into the ground and the last ice into Williams Lake.

It is usually in late April or early May when, while walking my dog, I discover the rose hip flowers. Every spring anew, I dare to approach one of the many thorny bushes and pick a few of the pale pink or winter-white flowers. I know the shoots will fight like clawed fingers reaching out, scratching my arms bloody. I know when put in a vase, the roses will wilt miserably within a day. Still, even for the few hours they last, I must have some on the dining room table, so that I can breathe in the rosy perfume.

Outside, the petals also fall off within a couple of weeks. But the real treat is yet to come. The treats that I am waiting for are the berry-sized rose hip pods. I have read that the further north they grow, the more vitamin C they contain. I believe it.

It takes the summer for the spent flowers to mature into crimson fruits. And it will take patience to wait for the right time to harvest these harbingers of fall. In this area, I was told, it is the morning after the first frost. However, if that happens too late in the season, rose hip maggot flies will have gotten there first. Timing is everything.

To get ready, I slip into worn-out jeans and a faded, long-sleeved cotton shirt. As soon as the early rising September sun's rays hit the trees, the temperature warms considerably. I will be greatly overdressed on this beautiful "Indian summer" day. My reason for dressing like a scarecrow is because the best fruits hang deep inside the gnarly branches and I'd rather sacrifice old clothing than my skin. Grabbing my banged-up aluminum pails, I venture out—alone.

Frankly, I ran out of friends to ask. For the first years, many accompanied me—once. Then they declined my invitation. "You're crazy," they'd say, "it takes forever to pick them and are such tedious work to process." This is true.

But thinking of the finished jelly, herbal tea, and soft candies, I place the pails on the dirt path, and start plucking from the first bush. The rose hips feel perfect, heavy and firm, and the hollow sound of them hitting the empty bucket is soon gone as the pods fill up in my containers. I hum a tune.

From time to time, I peek behind my shoulders or move cautiously around the shrub to reassure I am still the only one picking. After all, bears feed on the healthy food as well.

Besides the extremely high content of vitamin C, rose hips also contain beta-carotene, bioflavonoid, and pectin. Rose hips supposedly help lowering saturated fats, control blood pressure, and are good for the heart. If picking these gems makes me crazy, I don't mind being a little mad.

Okay, I admit it. I might have gone overboard once when experimenting by serving steamed seed balls as vegetables. The hairy-pulp mixture tasted like play dough and once swallowed, left an itch in the throat that made us cough like chain-smokers when waking up in the morning. This episode, not my shiniest culinary invention, got filed away in my brain with the comments written in capital red letters—DNR (*do not repeat*).

The memory makes me smile as I fill the third bucket. My hands and even my cheeks are scratched and one sleeve of my shirt is torn. I place the lids on my containers, and, reassured that I left plenty of fruits for good karma, I head home.

As children, I remember being assaulted with rose hips on our way to school. Boys would rip the sheaths open, sneak behind us girls, and drop them down our sweaters' pulled out collars. We screamed while the culprits ran off, laughing. The loose hairs and seeds would itch like crazy; the more we moved, the worse it got.

Now at home, I clean my bounty. Then I cut the rose hips in half, even though it is not absolutely necessary (and afterward it will take me days to scrub my fingernails clean), I do it for several reasons.

First of all, they dehydrate faster.

Secondly, later, when making a tasty cup of tea, the pieces soften quicker as the hot water seeps into the shells. Still, the steeping time is about ten minutes. I like to add a bit of honey and sometimes a few drops of lemon juice or a slice of fresh ginger to my brew.

The rose hips that I cook for jelly or candy also soften easier when cut in half. I boil the pods, covered with water, for an hour. After sifting the juice through a cheese cloth, I press and twist the cloth around the now mushy pulp, pressing out every last drop.

For the jelly, I measure one to one, extract and sugar and cook it like any other jelly or jam recipe, adding pectin, as well as a teaspoon of lemon or lime juice.

When the full canning jars, covered with a towel, are neatly lined up on my arborite countertop, I get busy washing pots and pans. The popping sound of the lids being pulled in is as satisfying to me as listening to classical music.

Finally, for the sweetest treat, the candies, I double the sugar and cooking time, before pouring the thick syrup onto a full-sized, with parchment lined, baking tray. At least twenty-four hours of drying time is needed. Cut into cubes they make tasty treats. Dipped in icing sugar and wrapped in cellophane, they make exquisite gifts.

Tea, jelly, and candies, all made from free rose hips, no wonder I smile when I smell them in the spring.

Family Meetings

"HOW LONG DO we have to sit here?" asked Oliver, fidgeting on his kitchen chair. He was seven years old.

Willy opened a green notebook.

"Is this necessary?" I asked. "This is not a boardroom."

"Yes, I think it is." He wrote the date on the top right corner. "I declare this meeting open. Does anybody have anything to say?"

Looking at each other, nobody spoke.

I don't remember where the idea of family meetings came from. We probably heard it from some other parents. What I do remember is how awkward the first Sunday evening session was.

Charlotte Diamond's faint "Four hugs a day . . ." penetrated from one of the children's bedrooms. *How were we supposed to do this? This was a bad idea. The kids are way too young.*

Oliver, dangling his legs back and forth, asked, "What do you want us to say? And how much longer is this meeting going to last?"

"Until it is adjourned."

Melanie, who was six years old and barely tall enough to reach the table without a booster seat, asked, "What's 'adjourned'?"

Willy explained the word adjourned and then he suggested, "Let's start with a bug."

"A bug?" echoed the kids in unison, straightening up.

"As in, what's bugging us?" I picked up Willy's train of thought. "I have a bug," I said, "I don't appreciate it when any of you come into the house with your dirty shoes on."

"When I'm working outside and all I need is a glass of water," Willy answered, "I don't want to waste time loosening shoe laces, slip out of my boots only to tie them up again half a minute later."

"I understand that. But you drag dirt all over the carpets and I have to clean it up."

"What can we do about it?"

Oliver took the bait. "Maybe we can put a glass of water beside the door," he suggested, "and when Daddy is thirsty, he doesn't have to come into the house."

"We have a motion," Willy said. "We're in business." He wrote: "Place a glass of water by the door."

Family meetings felt different from our communication during the week when we often crouched down to the kids' level, explaining things or—scolding them. Sitting around the table made each family member equal. Oliver and Melanie understood that their concerns were taken seriously and that they had a voice and a vote:

"Oliver doesn't like it when Melanie calls him spaghetti-arms."
"Don't be a buttinsky."
"Turn the radio-volume down."

When, after a few weeks, we felt the tone became too negative, we made a rule to start the meetings with a compliment:

"Oliver liked his birthday party."
"Congratulations to Melanie for learning to tell time."
"The Christmas tree looks beautiful."

Taking minutes was an excellent idea after all, as we often referred back to how specific issues had been settled. We took turns in writing. When the kids were secretaries, the meetings lasted long enough to break for ice cream as almost everything had to be spelled out.

With time, our discussions matured. We negotiated chores and pets. We progressed to major issues:

"Pocket money to be paid every Sunday night."

We made family decisions:

"Today we start saving for Disneyland."

When trampolines became the "in" thing, Oliver (twelve) and Melanie (eleven) wanted one too. Willy and I offered to contribute half the cost of a trampoline from the household allowance, if Oliver and Melanie came up with the other half.

Oliver whined, "Gordon Hicks's parents bought their kids a trampoline."

"And so did Susie Wickers's parents," Melanie echoed, adding, "and they get much more pocket money."

"We are the Bergers!" Willy trumpeted, standing up. Wagging his index finger, he said, "Do not compare us with the Hicks, the Wickers, or the Jones." He sat back down, "Now, back to business. Let's make a plan."

We disclosed our household budget and, together, searched for ways to cut our monthly expenses. Oliver and Melanie agreed to take on extra chores and a paper route. I remember vividly how proud our kids were, when, twelve months later, they paid for the trampoline at Canadian Tire. I also remember the smile of the sales clerk, who counted the plastic bag full of loose change.

A couple years later, our topics during meetings included bullying, drugs, and birth control. We debated curfews, after-school-jobs, and driving lessons. We even enjoyed serious "adult" discussions, compared pros and cons about Willy returning to school, and changing his career. With *Much Music* penetrating from Oliver's bedroom, we laughed about the one thing we could never agree on: the endurable volume-level of music.

By the time Oliver and Melanie were in high school, we decided to purchase a bigger house. It became the perfect opportunity to discuss mortgages and setting realistic financial boundaries. We made lists of "wants" and "needs." Forfeiting the temptation of a swimming pool we chose a home with an extra bedroom.

Now, we are content empty nesters. We listen to classical music or to no music at all. Oliver is twenty-seven years old, a wise money manager and a homeowner and Melanie is twenty-six years old, has a university degree, and is globetrotting, using her own savings.

Family meetings are one of the better things we implemented, and if we could do it over again, we would start even earlier.

First published in *Back Home*

Never Say Never

"NEVER," PREDICTED OUR neighbors, shaking their heads, "never will people drive seventeen kilometers out of town for a garage sale."

For a month prior to the gigantic sale in June 1989, my husband shamelessly advertised our yard sale to everybody and anybody. Willy even managed to get our preschooler daughter and second-grader son all worked up. I overheard Oliver and Melanie planning the spending of their dreamed fortune. Looking at their display of rock collections, broken crayons, Teddy Ruxpin's balloon, and one hugged-to-shreds Care Bear, I warned Willy, "You're setting them up for a huge disappointment."

Undeterred, he dragged several pieces of plywood, pressed boards and paneling, whatever he could find in our sheds, outside. He snapped the lids off his in town purchased glossy white and red paint canisters, unwrapped a new brush and slabbed a coat of white on the boards as background. Then, above his scarlet painted arrows, pointing the way, he wrote: "Moving Sale," "Keep going," "This is the way," "You're almost there."

"You have to spend money to make money," he said with a smug grin on his face.

"You should advertise it properly," I smirked back, "and call it junk sale."

In my opinion, all the rubble Willy had collected over the years, the mismatching tire-rims, the loosely rolled up second-hand barbed wire, the three kitchen chairs of which one had no back left, and all the rest of it, belonged not in a sale, but in the dump.

On second thought, let me rephrase that. All of it except the washing machine. Willy "found" it four years ago in the landfill. After washing the washing machine, pun intended, and replacing the timer for sixty dollars, which was equivalent to a week's grocery money—and to me it was gambling in the highest degree—it has been working like a charm. It was one of the few things not up for sale.

Ever since we had moved onto our ten-acre lot and built this hobby farm ten years ago, Willy had accumulated and hoarded stuff from work, leftover building materials, and collectables (his opinion) from the refuse. Some weeks, he returned more loaded from the landfill than when he had left. But organized and clean he was. Lumber was stored on shelves, sorted by sizes, tools neatly bunched together and kept dry, jars and buckets cleanly rinsed. And when he ran out of storage, he promptly constructed a new outbuilding.

Now, Saturday morning at six-thirty, dressed in jackets and boots, Willy and I carried, from sheds to yard, piles of twenty-gallon plastic buckets and oodles of one-gallon glass jars Willy had salvaged from his cooking job at Savalas Steak House in Williams Lake.

Oliver and Melanie crafted a table on which they displayed their goods and intended to sell refreshments. As our German shepherd, Max, ran confused back and forth, Willy and I arranged our merchandise in front of the dew-sparkling grass along both sides of our driveway. The trees threw shadows on tires, crates, wooden pallets, flower pots with and without content, shovels, spades, some with broken handles, rakes with missing spikes, chimney-cleaning tools, gardening hoses, watering cans, a leaking two-men tent, canvas, tarp, and axes. Everything that wasn't nailed down was for sale: troughs, home-made rabbit cages, and rainwater holding tanks.

"Crazy", I thought, schlepping the crib to the end of our lined-up goods and placing it beside the high chair and three boxes with baby clothes "all these once vital goods had become unnecessary baggage."

Life in town was going to be different. There was no garden or animals to look after. Oliver and Melanie could sign up for any extracurricular activity without the carpooling worry. I might work part-time.

That job prospect was my excuse to get rid of the canning supplies. Except for making jam and jelly, I never truly got the hang of preserving and pickling, like my Canadian neighbours. After placing pots and jars outside, I pushed my cold hands into my jacket pockets heading toward the house.

The frenzy about this garage sale was shear madness. I made it clear to my family, other than lending a hand during the preparations, I was not going to participate. I refused to humiliate myself by asking money from decent people for our trash.

"Never," I said aloud while back in the kitchen shortly past seven, I began cooking breakfast. According to the advertisement Willy had placed in the Tribune, our sale was scheduled from 9-2, or until all was sold, whichever came first. Assuming people actually would follow the last-night's planted signs from the 150 Mile House turn off all the way to our house.

I heard the front door open and footsteps stomping through the boot room. Willy, followed by his little assistants, entered the kitchen.

"Hmm, that coffee smells heavenly," he said.

Pouring the brew into two mugs, I said, "You still have to price everything. How will you manage?"

"We're ready," said Willy looking at the kids. "Right guys?"

"Ready," they sang in unison, grabbing for toast and peanut butter.

"We're not pricing anything," Willy explained, "My strategy is to allow customers' the pleasure of bartering."

I said nothing. Why should I? I wasn't going to be outside. But my thoughts went berserk: What did my husband know about garage sales in the first place? Growing up, this concept had been as foreign to us as getting lost in a forest, fist-fights at hockey games, or Northern Lights. Since living in Canada, we had strolled through a few such sales, where items had been price-tagged. What made him think he could change the rules? What made him the expert all of a sudden?

Willy placed his empty cup and plate in the sink and disappeared into the bedroom. I was mixing the kids' lemonade for their wobbly stand when Max started barking.

"Somebody's here," I called down the hallway. "Come quick. I'm not going out there." Lifting the horizontal plastic blinds at the kitchen window I peeked out. Max barked wildly up our fir tree by the middle shed.

"I don't see anybody," I said and hurried with the kids in tow through the boot-room and out the front door. When I saw what the racket was about, I shoved the children back inside as quickly as I could and banged the door shut.

"A bear, a bear!" Melanie screamed.

Willy came running into the boot-room.

"There's a bear on the tree," I cried. "Now we have to call the whole thing off."

"Hold your horses. Don't get so excited," Willy said. He fetched the camera from the shelf, opened the door and clicked away at the animal hugging our tree trunk about ten-feet above our charged up dog. Then Willy called Max and as soon as he retreated, the black bear slid down and disappeared into the bush.

"Not to worry," Willy said, closing the lens of the camera.

For the first time, I noticed Willy wearing his ripped lumber jacket and a pair of wrinkled, dirty pants he must have retrieved from the laundry.

"You're not wearing *that*, are you?"

"Yep."

"You look frumpy."

"Good." Willy put the camera away. "I don't want to give the impression we're rich."

He reached for his shoes and sat on the bench by the door. Winking at his helpers, he said, "We're going to make money today." He tied his shoe laces. "Remember sales people, everything must go."

Oliver and Melanie nodded enthusiastically, slipping their jackets back on.

"It's only eight o'clock." As I said it, we heard the first vehicle coming up our quarter-mile driveway.

Willy jumped up and clapped his hands. "Let's go."

Oliver and Melanie followed with pitcher and plastic cups in hand.

I returned to the kitchen. At my spy spot, the window above the kitchen sink, I watched the lady from one of the second hand stores in Williams Lake walk up and down the yard like a sergeant on a mission. In less than three minutes, she had gathered the two baby-sized life jackets, the geranium arrangement, the crib, the high chair, and all the good stuff. Willy and she talked for a bit. My husband opened his hand, accepted bills, stuffed them into his jacket pocket, rubbed his hands, and helped her load.

Our entire stock of nonchipped, nonripped, or otherwise not-yet-worn-out items was gone, and our sale hadn't even officially started. Shaking my head, I got busy washing the dishes, making beds, and scrubbing the toilet. Pleased with our disinfectant-smelling bathroom,

I went back to the kitchen, spying through discretely separated blinds. It was nine'o clock.

My eyes grew at the sight. The yard was a bustling, dust-whirling market plaza. Hoards of people filed from cars and trucks that stood hastily parked in between the trees at the corner of our driveway. One lady, already on her way out, unlocked the door of her station wagon. She had a long, heavy chain thrown over her shoulder. I cracked open the window. Laughter and bits of conversations reached my ears: "Wasn't that a crazy long drive?" "Crazy!" "Odd, no prices." "We came from town." "Always one more sign . . ." "Kept going . . ." "Ha-ha sure was worth it."

The moment a customer picked up an item, Willy was there chatting them up. The person nodded, reached into his pocket, Willy stretched out his hand—over and over.

From time to time, I scanned the bush, but thank heaven, the bear was nowhere to be seen. More cars arrived. One man carried away white plastic buckets piled-up twice his own height. He deposited them by his vehicle and came back to fetch their lids. Many held lemonade cups in their hands. Business was booming, even for our children.

Suddenly, a wave of nostalgia overcame me. Melanie and Oliver had enjoyed six and seven years of complete freedom out here, playing in dirt and snow, having pigs, goats, rabbits, cats, and dogs for friends. Now we started a new chapter. We did what we swore, only a couple years ago, we'd never do, move into the fly ash filled air of Williams Lake. Scarier still was the bigger mortgage we signed on. With interest rates at fifteen percent, was it the right time for a move like ours?

I didn't know it then, but we were living the typical European immigrant life, purchasing isolated, rural property, enjoying space, and privacy we hadn't known growing up, only to sell and move back into civilization a few years later.

Melanie, coming into the kitchen, ripped me out of my reverie.

"Mami," she said handing me the empty pitcher, "One granny gave us one dollar and didn't want any change back."

"How do you know she was a granny?" I asked while filling the jug with water.

"I'm sure she is a granny. She's old and she was very nice," she said, stirring in the crystals with a wooden spoon.

"Yes, I am sure then, she must be a granny."

Melanie took the jug and trotted busily back outside.

I felt once again, a slight stab of guilt for denying our children growing up around grandparents, aunts, or uncles. For our children, relatives were flawless figments of their imaginations. How deep can a little family of four plant their roots?

Once more, I investigated through the kitchen window. Willy pulled out a wad of bills from his shirt pocket, sorted it, and stashed it inside his jeans. Sun rays shone like spotlights onto the shrinking moving sale display. Still more cars, drove up. People now were dressed lighter with T-shirts and short-sleeved blouses. One lady picked up our one-legged wooden seat—our milking stool.

"Yeah, right," I said aloud, "just what you need."

Willy went over, talked to her. He took her money, slid it into his shirt pocket. The lady smiled and walked away with her purchase.

"That's it," I said, let the blinds slip back into place and went into the bedroom to change into my coveralls with the deep pockets.

Seeking Normal

"THERE'S SOMETHING wrong in Oliver's head." I'm glad I finally verbalized it. I'm glad for the dimmed light in our bedroom.

"What do you mean?" asks Willy as he slips between the sheets.

"I don't know," I answer, fumbling with the duvet. "When I talk to him, sometimes, he doesn't answer me, doesn't register I'm speaking."

"He's a teenager," Willy scoffs. "What do you expect?"

"No, he's not. He's twelve." I turn off the light. "I'm telling you, something in his head is not right."

"You worry too much."

"I'm his mother. It's my job," I say.

A week earlier, at the beginning of October 1993, we had organized an "upside down" party for Oliver's birthday. His friends came, wearing their sweaters inside-out. The gifts were wrapped upside-down and the Mario Kart sponge cake was bottom-up. Everything about the fun-filled afternoon was upside-down. Afterward, I washed the dishes and vacuumed and life was supposed to return to normal.

Normal.

The first day back to school after Christmas, January 4, 1994, Oliver has trouble waking up. He sits at the breakfast table like a zombie.

I grab his shoulders, "Wake up, sleepyhead," I say, shaking him gently. "The holidays are over. Eat your toast."

He does, mechanically.

"Go brush your teeth."

He does. For ten minutes.

"Oliver, get dressed," I nag.

He does and then sits on the bed, staring at the carpet.

"Come on, buddy. What's wrong with you today? Let's go to school."

I follow him downstairs, help him into his down-filled winter coat, place his lunch box in his hands, and shove him out the door. The fresh air, I reason, will wake him up.

At work, I can't concentrate. I call the school to make sure Oliver has arrived. "Please keep an eye on him," I ask the teacher. "He wasn't himself this morning."

The phone call comes two hours later.

My coworker drives me to the hospital, where my husband is already waiting. Our boy's forehead is scratched and bloody and his lip cut. When he doesn't recognize me, I break down, bury my face in Willy's shirt.

Following doctors' orders, Oliver stays home from school for a week. I relay to his grade-six teacher what our family doctor had concluded: our son fainted in school because he has a virus.

Five days later, our family physician checks Oliver's reflexes, measures his pulse, and gives him a thumbs-up. Fidgeting on the chair in the examining room, I look at the doctor in his white coat, take a deep breath, and tell him about Oliver's absentmindedness.

"There's no ground for any further tests," he says.

"Something is off. I know it is."

The doctor winks at my son, who studies the poster on the ceiling with the snowboarder jumping over extreme cliffs, but speaks to me, "You told me Oliver is an artist?"

"Yes?"

"So he's probably just a little bit of a dreamer. That's all." He closes the file. "You worry too much."

"That's what my dad says," says Oliver.

Three months later, after the school Easter break, the morning scenario repeats itself. Oliver has trouble waking up and sits at the breakfast table like a zombie.

Melanie recognizes the signs too. "Mami, what's wrong with Oliver?"

"I am not sure, sweetie."

This time I drive my son to school. Tears run down my face as I leave him standing there, looking lost between the parking lot and the school entry. "You worry too much," I tell myself. "It was a virus. You're seeing things."

The phone call comes shortly before lunch.

Oliver looks at me from the hospital bed, his face pale, his eyes tired and watery. It stabs my heart. The pain feels good. Give me more; I want to suffer too.

I sit at his bedside and hold his hand.

My son smiles weakly. "Shit happens, Mom."

I look around to see if anybody heard and can't help but smile too.

Finally, we get a referral for an EEG (electroencephalogram) and make the six-hundred-kilometer trip to Vancouver a couple weeks later.

At BC Children's Hospital, we are told, "It could be worse," and given pamphlets, "What is Epilepsy?" *Apparently, four million people in North America have epilepsy. Alfred Nobel had epilepsy. Dan Glover has epilepsy.*

"Patrick, our Irish neighbour had epilepsy", I think. "He is dead."

We hand out the medical brochures to Oliver's teachers, friends, and their parents. We order a medical bracelet. There are no support groups within the next four hundred kilometers of where we live. We know only one other family with a son suffering from this disorder. His mother tells me to keep records on our boy's progress and setbacks, medication intakes, and side effects.

Our son's new name at school is "seizure salad". We get a dog for Oliver because most of his friends stop coming to our house. Buddy is a blissful puppy, curious and adventurous.

But Buddy runs off all the time. When I leave for work, I have to tie him to a post. When Oliver comes home from school, he frees his buddy, feeds him, and plays with him. They are each other's heroes—friends without prejudice.

I have become the ever-nagging mother. "Did you take your pills?"

Oliver hates taking his pills.

If an epileptic forgets one single dose of anticonvulsant medication, drug levels in the bloodstream plummet to the person's subtherapeutic zone. It takes days to bring these medication levels back up to safe range.

"Did you take your pills?"

My boy's eyes change. He stops smiling. His comb is full of hair. Oliver keeps losing his medical bracelet. Within a year, he expands from a size 10 to a size 16. At school, he falls asleep. At home he crouches on the floor in a fetal position, holding his stomach, rocking and waiting for the cramps to subside. I kneel on the linoleum floor beside him, cup his head against my chest so he can't see my face, and caress his blond curls. His hair smells so sweet.

I beg the medical experts to reduce the prescription drugs. The EEG-test results still shows irregularities in the brain waves, confirms consistent absence seizures. But we are told we're lucky.

"The patient is not having grand mal seizures. The medication works. His blood level is normal," the neurologist at B.C. Children's Hospital explains. "Two years," he promises. "In two years the side effects will fade."

"Did you take your pills?"

Every morning at breakfast I force 125 mg of Valporic acid down my son's throat, knowing an hour later he will cramp up. Every evening, I supervise as he swallows twice that amount, hoping the night will let Oliver sleep in peace. He hangs his arm off the bed so his buddy, Buddy, can lick his hand.

"Did he take the pills?" "We're lucky." "It could be worse." "Two years." "Did he take the pills?" My lullabies. My nightmare.

During a hot summer week in August 1995, a friend invites Oliver to their family's boat-access-only cabin for a sleepover. Somebody's mom, at last, is not afraid. I am elated for my son, who eagerly packs his swimsuit and sleeping bag.

His medication lays forgotten on the bathroom counter.

There are basically two types of deadly accidents for people with epilepsy: driving and drowning.

An hour's drive from home, I knock on the door of Willy's work-colleague and plead with him to lend me his rowboat. Dusk lurks on the black lake while I struggle to find a rhythm with the paddles, zigzag much too slowly toward the cabin. The singing and laughing stop abruptly when I step out of darkness toward the crackling camp fire, my son and his teenage friends. The pill box cuts into the palm of my clenched fist.

"Your pills." I hand the small container to Oliver and smile at the small group of annoyed boys who, holding their sticks with melting marshmallows, stare back. "You forgot your pills," I repeat and without another word disappear the same way I came.

In 50 to 60 percent of cases, the cause of epilepsy is unknown.

A privately paid MRI deeply cuts into our savings, but puts our worries about a brain tumor to rest.

A naturopathic doctor tells us the accumulated mercury from Oliver's childhood vaccinations cause his seizures. But our son is not willing to follow strict diets and swallow, on top of his medication, a bunch of herbs.

A physiotherapist who specializes in Craniosacral therapy is convinced that the bump Oliver received on his head, playing cops and robbers in grade five, aggravated and malpositioned his cranium. But he warns, "You best don't mention this visit to your physician."

The psychologist we consult assures us that our son handles his fate like a pro. "His mother on the other hand . . ."

Our rainy-day fund is greatly overdrawn by the time we fly to Switzerland in December 1995. In Zürich, at the Schweizerische Epilepsie Klinik, a German specialist compliments me on my record keeping, which helps him confirm many facts we already know—and some we don't.

> Oliver, male, fourteen, has primary generalized epilepsy with juvenile absences. The patient has unfortunately experienced significant side effects from medications and has been reluctant to use them. Since the diagnosis, he has suffered five tonic-clonic seizures, with the last one being the most severe, leaving him with observable memory impairment. Cranial nerve examination is normal. Blood tests show a high level of serum concentration; a carefully monitored reduction in medication is advisable. A cerebral magnetoencephalography should be considered.

The chance for Oliver to outgrow his epilepsy is unlikely, the possibility to pass it onto his children, remote.

"Thank you for coming all this way. Please feel free to stay in touch."

On Oliver's sixteenth birthday, he gets his driver's license. Despite doctors' dark predictions, we hope he might have outgrown his epilepsy. Gradually and carefully, he is weaned off the medication.

Six months later he suffers a severe grand-mal seizure while working behind the service counter at McDonald's. The ambulance medical team picks Oliver up and, with screeching sirens, they rush to the hospital.

A new medication is slowly introduced, increased to 100 mg of Lamotrigine a day. He must give up his driver's license for one year. Again, my boy, and forever my baby, suffers from stomach cramps and extreme fatigue.

Since our new public transit was still very limited to routes and schedules, I drive him to and from the Williams Lake Power Plant, where he works as a sweeper. On weekends, I chauffeur Oliver to his girlfriend's house. Then I drive them to the movies and two hours later, I pick them up. Finally, back at the girlfriend's house, I wait in the car while, in the shadow of the porch light, they kiss each other good-night.

Shortly after graduation in 1999, Oliver receives a one year work visa for Australia. At the Royal Inland Hospital in Vancouver—having outgrown the privilege to be consulted at BC Children's Hospital—our son is reevaluated and receives a medical report, which he will pack with his medication and his clothes. Our son leaves home with the same eagerness we had emigrated from Switzerland twenty years earlier.

Buddy stays with us.

When, six months later, we fly "Down Under" for a visit, Oliver proudly shows us his surfboard, tours us around Surfer's Paradise. He doesn't look good. He doesn't take his pills. He parties. He smokes.

Together we travel south along the coast and then head inland to Thredbo, where for the next three months he will work and snowboard.

I notice absent seizures. "Oliver, you are headed into a grand mal. I know it."

"Don't worry mom. I'm okay."

"What if you have a seizure while snowboarding?" I ask. "You could kill yourself."

"Oh mom," he hugs me, "then I die doing what I love to do."

I hold back tears. "You can say that when you're eighty. Not now."

With the heaviest heart, my husband and I board the plane to fly back to Canada. For the next months, we receive regular letters and e-mails. In them, our son doesn't write about his generalized seizures. He doesn't write about waking up with a groggy head and a cigarette-burnt hole in the carpet beside his cold Marlboro butt. All this he tells us only once he is home again.

Oliver moves into his own apartment with Buddy. Our son is twenty years old, old enough to make decisions: The medication's unbearable side effects versus the small chance of a seizure are worth trying to lead a healthy lifestyle without swallowing drugs. But he looks pale. He works shifts at one of our lumber mills. He smokes cigarettes and occasionally, he drinks beer.

I hear the ambulance across town. When the phone call comes, I rush to the hospital's emergency ward. Once again, Oliver lays, limp and pale, on the white emergency room bed with the blue curtain—superficial privacy—pulled. The smell of vomit and bleach and the sight of my baby and his frightened looking girlfriend by his side make me feel faint.

A young emergency doctor examines Oliver. "Where did it happen?" he asks.

His girlfriend uses all her strength not to cry, "In his living room."

"How long was he unconscious?"

She guesses, "Maybe about seven minutes."

Behind the curtain, someone moans. I want to scream at him to shut up. The physician and I exchange looks. A nurse opens the curtain, comes in and checks the intravenous.

Deliberately slowly the doctor says, "It might not have been a seizure."

Oliver opens his eyes and groggily answers, "It was."

"It might not have been a seizure," I repeat loudly, trying to make eye contact with Oliver.

But he repeats, "It was. I know how it feels."

After promising the doctor to keep close watch on him, I am allowed to take Oliver home. In his old room, I sit and watch my son, a young man, lying between his *Star Wars* sheets. He sleeps for many hours. Leaning over his sweaty hair, I kiss his forehead. His hair smells musky and manly.

Oliver wakes up and says, "Shit happens, Mom."

Today it isn't funny. Not even a little bit.

He closes his eyes again, slips back into the place of darkness.

Tomorrow, he will face his new normal. For the following weeks, he won't remember going to the movies with his girlfriend or what he did at work the previous day. For the next year, his body will—yet again—struggle to adjust to the side effects of his new drug Keppra, which will cost him more than his monthly car payment. Because he wasn't alert enough to grab the lifeline that the emergency doctor tried to throw him, this episode will officially be recorded. As if having a tonic-clonic seizure is a criminal offence, his driver's license will be revoked for one year.

But Oliver is lucky.

As long as—no matter how tired they make him—he takes the pills twice a day every day, as long as he doesn't touch any other drugs, as long as he doesn't drink alcohol. *(One drink of alcohol increases the chance of a seizure by ten percent, three drinks by eighty-five percent.)* As long as he gets enough sleep, as long as he keeps a regular job without shift work and without too much overtime, as long as he doesn't participate in extreme sports, as long as he doesn't smoke (he tries), and as long as he doesn't consume sugar and caffeine—he can lead a normal life.

Normal?

Three years ago, in the spring of 2006, Oliver asked me to accompany him to a workshop, offered by the Northern Health and The Center for Epilepsy and Seizure Education in British Columbia. We spent the weekend together, learning and crying. Crying for things we did wrong because we didn't know better.

An internationally renowned epilepsy expert, who came all the way from California, taught us, among other stunning revelations, about medication dosages, the therapeutic ranges and levels which can't be measured by weight alone but differ for each patient. We learned about toxic and subtherapeutic consequences of too much or too little medication. I regret deeply having forced what I understand now as being too high a dosage of pills on my son.

We learned that Oliver's type of epilepsy is not operable. But it's okay. Oliver found his normal.

At twenty-seven, he is in good, physical shape; he looks and lives healthy. He shares his own house with a wonderful girlfriend and his ailing Buddy. He still takes Keppra, but works at a day job full time and volunteers as ski patrol at the local ski hill. Oliver has been seizure free for four years. He is indeed very lucky. He is lucky to have survived his rebellious years.

One percent of the population has or has had some type of epileptic seizure. Due to the stigma around this disorder of the central nervous system and the severe side effects of the medication, many will not seek treatment.

JOHNNY THE TIPPER

MY FATHER'S FRIENDS called him Johnny the tipper. He was never a wealthy man and, more often than not, he worked two jobs to feed his family of six. However, when it came to tipping, my dad was as generous as Santa Claus. At restaurants, he would order a one-litre-bottle of pop to be shared among the four of us children just so there would be enough money left for a generous gratuity.

"Don't order, if you can't tip 15 percent," Dad taught us.

From him, we learned how to calculate percentage: "Move the decimal one number to the left and you have ten percent, divide that in half and add the two together. If the number is uneven, round it up, never down."

Growing up in an orphanage, my Dad had been ostracized by his community. He was forced to fight for everything, even the basic right to occupy a desk at school. I think that's why he needed to make others smile, feel respected, and appreciated.

Not only did my father leave extra money at every restaurant, he also tipped the shoemaker and his barber (probably as an apology for only having half a head of hair). Even for the employee at the gas station, my dad always had an extra coin. And I am sure he slipped a tip into the man's hand from whom he and his buddies rented the bowling lane once a week.

To the ridicule of my family and friends, I can't help myself but do my father proud. It doesn't matter if a waitress is testy or a waiter not around when needed, I will find a reason for them to deserve a tip. After all, people are entitled to have a bad day once in a while and if we, the customers, are granted a chance to make someone's imperfect day a little bit better, shouldn't we at least give it a try?

When, as a young family, we went out for dinner, I would be anxious for my husband to be generous when the time came to settle the bill. Sometimes, he didn't pay the fifteen percent that I concluded we owed.

Our kids knew how to push my buttons.

"Dad, I don't think we got very good service. We vote for no tip to the server," my son would tease.

"Yeah, look at his shoes, they are not shiny enough" or, "Her hair is all tied up, what's up with that," my daughter would badger.

Always caught, I would then launch into my list of all the positive things the waiter or waitress did. We'd debate back and forth until my final argument, "Don't order if you can't tip 15 percent."

My children's current opinion on gratuities has greatly "tipped" toward my point of view, as they're both employed in the service industry now. My girlfriend, however, has not been so easily convinced.

She invited me for lunch the other day. I have to admit that we got, what appeared to be, a rather snippy waitress. First she refused to let us sit beside the window even though every single table was free. She looked as if she was going to start crying at any moment and forgot the simplest things, such as bringing us water or asking if we would like coffee after lunch.

"She deserves no tip," my friend said.

"She needs extra; don't you see how upset she is?"

My friend insisted, "She's not doing a good job, therefore she deserves no tip."

"You don't know why she's so upset," I argued. "Maybe her mother died."

"If her mother had died, she would have time off to be at the funeral."

"Maybe her boyfriend dumped her," I insisted.

"You're crazy." Throwing up her arms, my girlfriend said, "Okay then, let's ask her why she's such a grump."

That said, my lunch date got up from her chair and approached the bar where our waitress was standing. They talked for a while, my friend started to smile, and then the waitress's face also relaxed. Finally, they hugged.

My friend returned to our table. "Nicole is six weeks pregnant" she told me. "She is extra sensitive to light and smell and can't keep any food down. It is very hard for her to serve, but she can't afford to take time off."

"See," I gloated, "I have just proven my point. She does deserve extra and she will be thankful to you for your generosity."

My girlfriend still thought a minimum amount was appropriate. She was happy for the pregnancy, but Nicole had a job to do and did not perform it well. The idea of a compassionate tip made no sense to my lunch mate.

Sometimes, I feel that maybe my father did exaggerate in teaching me about gratuity and generosity. Maybe everybody else is right. But for some reason, it doesn't matter to me. If out of a hundred servers, one has as good a reason for having a bad day as Nicole did, it will do for me. I am who I am. After all, I am Johnny the tipper's daughter.

Broadcasted on *CBC First Person Singular*

Home Sweet Home

WHEN WE PLAN a visit to Switzerland, our families think of it as: "They're coming home."

As emigrants, we feel pressure to make our families understand that we made the right decision in leaving and that we are a happy family living the Canadian dream.

Two weeks before our departure, I take drastic measures: doubling up on dental-whitening-strips, getting a funky haircut, and buying flattering clothes. We fill our suitcases with smoked Pacific wild salmon, peanut butter, maple syrup and dream catchers.

When we step out of the airplane in Zürich, the scenery and the language feel cozy. The Yodel music playing on the rental car radio makes me hum along.

However, I refuse to drive on the narrow roads with the industrious traffic. Even sitting beside my husband who is an excellent driver makes me dizzy. A sign at an intersection says to turn the engine off when the traffic light is red. The second it turns green everyone speeds off. Horns blow and fingers point toward my husband, who is still fiddling with the engine key.

At the family reunion I realize that my funky hairstyle is conservative here and my new clothes are yesterday's fashion. But everybody is happy to see us. We all have earned a few new wrinkles, since our last gathering eight years ago. I can relax.

Then, Aunt Heidi asks, "So how does it feel to be home?"

"Home," I say with a sigh and a smile, "is in Canada."

Even while surrounded by family, some things just don't fit anymore. We come from different worlds and different cultures. We are tourists in our old country.

As much as we love white asparagus, bratwurst, roesti, fondue, and linzer torte, it is impossible to arouse enough of an appetite for a five-course midday meal, especially in the still—before the turn of the century—cigarette-smoke polluted restaurants. Besides, our main meal in Canada is eaten at dinner time. All I usually crave for lunch is a little soup. Finally, the coffee here is so strong, it makes my hands tremble and twists my stomach.

When mailing postcards to our friends back in Canada, we try to find the lineup at the post office—the way we remember it—until we realize that now one has to pick a number.

Every item in the stores now has two price tags, one for the value in Euro and the other for the value in Swiss Franks. And while I am on the subject: the prices are outrageous! However, we figure we are on holiday and pull out our credit cards; after all, "buy now, pay later" is the North American motto.

We learn that it is no longer correct to purchase a ticket and hop on the train like we used to do. Before boarding, we must stamp the ticket in a bright orange validation machine. The sophisticated train system in Switzerland works like their impeccable watches: punctual and reliable. If a person arrives one minute late, the train is gone.

In the region, where I live, people are perpetually fifteen minutes late. We call it Cariboo time. Needles to say, it created a slight problem during our visit.

In Zermatt, a German couple (not Swiss) graciously explains to us, which gondolas to board to reach the twelve thousand-foot peak of the Little Matterhorn. From the top station, we climb (slowly because we feel light-headed) onto an enclosed balcony and are stunned by the view. We look over the snow-covered Alps that swim in an ocean of clouds. The sun feels close enough to touch. I fervently watch the silent symphony of peaks and valleys. For a few minutes my memory fits.

Two weeks into our holiday, my head aches from the cigarette smoke in all the public places. The yodeling gets on my nerves and I can't wait to leave. Promising to return soon, I accept the usual bag of hand-me-down clothes from my sister for which my girlfriends in Canada will envy me.

When Air Canada flies over the Coastal Mountains before it lands on our small Williams Lake airport runway, I feel that I am coming home.

Here, I merrily cruise down the road in my Honda with a sticker that reads: "I am Canadian." Here, I fit—until I meet someone new who says, "Hi, nice to meet you. Um . . . your accent . . . where're you from?"

First published in *Spotlight*

THONG IS WRONG, ISN'T IT?

I TOOK THE FIRST piece of underwear out of the glossy cardboard box and my fingers dropped it as if it had caught on fire. I had bought g-strings by mistake. Too embarrassed to return the package to Costco for a refund, I stuffed the tangled pieces of string underneath my other underwear in the drawer and—forgot about them.

The same week, Melanie, who was seventeen by now, sat on the balcony with a friend of hers. They were giggling and whispering.

"What's so funny?" I asked.

Then I saw what they saw. My sixty-five-year-old neighbor, Shirley, had hung up several thongs on her clothesline. The garbs, smaller than the pins, fluttered in the wind like the fluorescent plastic ribbons that I used in my vegetable garden to scare off the birds.

During our morning walk the next day, I asked Shirley about the thongs on her line. With her deep laughter she told me that it all started when, after cleaning out the basement, she washed and hung out rags and torn towels. Her other neighbor had made derogatory remarks about clothesline-contents revealing people's personalities.

"I felt provoked," she told me, "so, I was going to give them something worthwhile to talk about." Shirley took her g-strings, which until yesterday she had discreetly dried inside the house, and exhibited them on her clothesline.

"How courageous!" I laughed and confessed to her about the underwear that was tucked away at the bottom of my drawer.

"At first," Shirley explained, "they felt like flossing. But once you get used to them, you will never wear anything else."

I was not convinced and left mine untouched.

A few weeks later, as I picked up my geraniums from the nursery in town, my ears perked up when I heard the word "thong" amongst the ladies behind and in front of the counter.

"My daughter buys them with her own money," one customer said. "But I make them disappear as soon as I find them in the laundry basket."

"My daughter's g-strings were being exposed above her low-cut pants and the tattoo on her back," another mother said and went on talking, waving her hands, "and when I pointed this out to her", she snapped, "Duh."

A third mother laughed, "We should form a support group. MAT Mother's Against Thongs."

Obviously, there is a new fashion trend that we middle-aged mothers from rural communities haven't read about in *The Williams Lake Tribune* or *Home and Garden*.

These g-strings, though, must be popular because I found mini-panty-liners for thongs at the grocery store. They are available in white and black and consist of a fraction of liner for the same price as the regular ones. The manufacturers of feminine protection are making fortunes with the shrinking fashion of lingerie. "Mini" has never meant so much.

My daughter has also found out how comfortable g-strings are. The tiny bits of rope-like string, with a little triangle that I assumed was the front, appeared in my laundry. They were impossible to untangle, fold and/ or neatly pile up. To me, they look like asking for a permanent "wedgy".

There was only one way to find out.

I locked the bedroom door.

Pulling the strings up between my legs, careful not to tug too high and hurt myself, I arranged the top band around my waist. I slowly turned around, looked at my reflection and saw snow-white. But not Snow White.

"Thong is wrong!" yelled the Japanese wrestler in my bedroom mirror.

Thongs. What does that word mean anyway? Why plural? Certainly not for the quantity of fabric.

Thong: *Leather strip used for fastening heavy boots, the leather lashes of a whip.*

It sounds to me like we are going back to medieval times. Is the goose still so intent on impressing the gander? It worries me. What's next?

This is where the story ended, two weeks ago, before my trip to the small shopping center in town. In one of the shop windows, a cute pair of capri pants caught my eyes and I entered the store. Inside, there were only a few left on the rack. "Try them on, get it over with, they won't fit anyway," I told myself.

They fit—like a glove.

I placed hanger and pants on the glass counter. The thoughtful summer student behind the cash register suggested, between chewing her gum, "With these tight-fitting capri we advise for you to wear thongs," conveniently producing, from underneath the counter-display, a blister pack with a rather sexy picture on it. "They don't show the panty-line, you know."

I looked at her with an all-knowing smirk, raised my eyebrows and smiled. "I already have some at home."

First read at *The Banff Centre Writing with Style*

The Price

I COULD FILL A book with stories about visitors.

The "special" visitors' topic is a common dinner-conversation over a cheese raclette or a summer barbeque with our immigrant friends. Spinning episodes, we crow over whose unexpected drop-ins were treated with the most finesse, toasting each other's stories with red wine, groans, and glee.

The irony is, in Switzerland, no one would dare show up unannounced at someone's home. Not even for coffee. It remains a mystery to us, why this Swiss courtesy-rule doesn't apply in foreign countries. Whether it is Canadian's outstanding reputation as hosts, or the illusion that we expatriates crave the company of old-country folks, we don't know. All we know is that they keep coming. One after another, they find us.

Once, a friend of a friend of a schoolmate of Willy's brother called—collect—from the Greyhound station in Williams Lake. He needed to be picked up and housed until his money-transfer from Switzerland came through. This thirty-year-old stranger was on a world-tour with a small backpack and his little black address-book. He bragged to us that, so far, during his tramping through Europe and Asia, he hadn't paid for one single hotel stay.

For a week, he let himself be served as if our house was a five-star resort; he didn't even clear his own dishes from the table. Desperate to encourage his departure, Willy bought him his bus ticket to Quebec, where his little black book led him next.

Another time, a girlfriend of an elementary-school friend of mine showed us so little respect, she would not even consider our request to take her cigarette and tin can, the make-shift ashtray, outside. Sitting in our living room, she puffed and polluted our air, the air our young children and we breathed in. When I encouraged her, on the fourth-or-so day, to lend me a hand in the kitchen, she leaned back in our recliner and said, "I'm on holidays."

We have our own private names for people like that. But to put it nicely, we categorize them under: the price we pay for living in such a beautiful country. Everybody wants to see it too.

Eventually, we learned to set exploitation boundaries, learned to say "no," even learned to literally kick people out on the spot.

So far, it has happened twice.

The warning: "You don't want Willy pressing you for 'a talk' in his office," must have gone around. Our surprise drop-ins have improved somewhat—emphasis on "somewhat."

Two young men, one a brother of a colleague of Willy's, the other unknown to us at his arrival, showed up unannounced for an overnight stay. They ended up sleeping on the hide-a-bed in the living room for a week, eating and drinking us almost into the poor house.

"We will never forget your kindness," they said as they finally packed their bags. "Call us next time you're in Switzerland and we'll find a way to repay you."

"That's great," we thought, "at least they appreciated what we did for them."

A year later, we were in Switzerland and took them up on their offer. We called. One was busy. The other arranged to meet us during his lunch-hour at a fancy restaurant. Our anticipation for a free meal was short lived, as after a friendly hello, he beckoned us to the coffee-shop section for a cup of java. He drank a beer and ate a pretzel and ran out before the waiter brought the bill.

Then there was the family of four—I don't even remember whose referral they were—who dropped in and holidayed at the "Berger's Inn" for ten days. Their toddlers were terrors, marking our walls with crayons, peeing on the carpet, and breaking Oliver and Melanie's toys without the parents making any apologies. On the last evening of their stay, they invited us all out for dinner.

"Let's go to a nice place," they philanthropically proposed.

When the time came to settle the tab, they had—oh dear—forgotten their wallets. Back at home, they made no attempts of reimbursing us.

These tricksters cost us nerves, house repairs, and forced the scheming of a defense plan to put in place *before* the next uninvited company stepped across our threshold. We resorted to lying. "We won't be home," we would tell them. Or, "That's too bad because we're just leaving on a holiday ourselves."

On the other side of the price tag, there are, for Willy and me, two dearly loved family members we invited many times, and for whom we would give anything could they come.

Willy's father stopped corresponding with us after we abdicated from the family butcher store in La Chaux-de-Fonds. Adding salt into the wound was our announcement that we had become Canadian citizens. A year-and-a-half into his silence, Willy's father died in a terrible car crash.

We took out a line of credit to fly to the funeral.

In the church, where we stood beside Willy's mom to receive wishes of condolences, my husband was accused, "Your father had to die for you to return."

I didn't know where Willy found his strength, but he kept answering to their not so thinly disguised barbs, "We are not staying."

Upon our return to Canada, the owner of the slaughterhouse where Willy worked had gone bankrupt. We were left minus the final, outstanding paycheck, no job, a house-mortgage, and the money we owed for our flight.

Still, for me, it was not the most desolate time. My most despairing days followed the phone call after my brother, Kurt, had suffered a massive heart attack. Kurt, who had accused me of betraying my country by leaving, lay in a deep coma. He was not expected to survive. I arrived in Zürich three days too late. My brother was only twenty-nine.

The price for living so far away—we pay physically, mentally and emotionally—is a hefty one. Our consolation, Willy's and mine, is to believe in our hearts, had they come, Willy's father and Kurt, they would have understood why we decided to settle and raise a family here. All others: sisters, Willy's brother, moms, my dad, aunts, uncles, did.

Over the years, most plan their holidays around our famous Williams Lake Stampede.

For the month of June, all Williams Lakers dig out and wear their western shirts and ten-gallon hats. Rodeo themes are painted on store windows. During the first long weekend in July, our population doubles with tourists and cowboys.

A parade and street party kick off the festivities. Local service clubs serve outdoor pancake breakfasts, and in the evening, steak and bean or rib dinners.

Each of the four days of rodeo competition begins, to the surprise of our visitors, with the singing of "Oh Canada." In Switzerland, the National Anthem is sung once a year, on the National day, and most people do not know the words to it. Here, before every performance, it touches me still, to stand up and belt out " . . . we stand on guard for thee . . .," with our visitors staring in awe.

For the next three hours, sitting on the narrow bleachers, I lean to the side and translate to our European guests the rodeo announcer's lively comments on the ladies barrel races, bareback and saddle bronc riding, the bull-riding, and the hilarious wild cow milking.

My proudest moment is during Williams Lake's unique mountain race. Once the horn blows, up to ten riders stampede down a steep hill. All spectators rise to their feet, hollering and screaming, watching as the horses slide and slip down the breakneck embankment, leaving clouds of dust behind. It is not uncommon for a rider to fall off his horse, or for a horse to take a tumble. Those who make it down to the track, race to finish in front of the grand stand and roaring crowd.

Everybody who first experiences the Williams Lake Stampede is mind-boggled at the glimpse of our wild west. All who come have the desire to return and see more of our home town and beyond.

And so, we seize the opportunity to show off our beautiful, forested Cariboo, Likely's little-known gold-rush town ruins, Chilcotin's grasslands, Farwell Canyon's sand dunes, Barkerville, and more. One summer, I even spent an incredible three weeks with my mom, driving north all the way to Yukon's Dawson city and back.

These superb memories, holidays for all of us, tip the cost balance from expenditure to reward—from price to prize.

NOW WHAT?

DURING THE HYPE of our daughter's upcoming graduation, I found myself in a huge void that forced me to reflect on my life.

This would be it. Melanie would graduate from high school and I, from motherhood. She would be honoured with certificates and bursaries; I wouldn't. She'd celebrate, bathe in gifts and glory; I'd pay for it. Finished with raising kids, it was too late for should haves and could haves. Now what? I had no career to focus on. My job had been to raise the family. There would be no more work, and I would be laid off.

I could become a devoted corporate wife, join the golf club, buy a membership at the health spa, work up a sweat, go for fancy lunches with Pepto-Bismol in my purse, become a regular at the beauty parlour, wax my legs and upper lips, and sign up for seminars on menopause. I could write my biography.

Or I can find a new purpose in my life. What are my qualifications? I raised a family: kids, pets, and "kept" a husband, i.e., marriage together, polished cooking, and washing and cleaning skills.

I have learned the true meaning of listening. It is done with the ears exclusively and not with my mouth, in fact, there are times to zip it, even when asked for advice from our young adult kids. I also know that eye contact is a must only when confronting a bank teller over a lost deposit, not necessarily beneficial, however, when conversing with a teenager about birth control. That and other such touchy subjects are preferably discussed while driving or doing dishes.

Furthermore, it is vital to keep good stock of staples on hand, such as pop, chips, double-double chocolate-chip cookies, and the latest board—today probably video—games. Whether it is kids, husband or dogs that test your patience, count to ten before throwing a fit.

To be competent with vehicles is another credential of mine. I have learned, anthropoids, including mechanically operated equipment, can't be verbally encouraged, talked into, or bribed into performing. Filling up gasoline is absolutely and without exception, necessary. Also, when feeling a sudden fight with the steering wheel, which is violently pulling to one side, there is a chance, one of the tires is flat and whoever needs to be dropped off or picked up will be late or not get there at all.

Finally, at home again, I know that if I am sitting on the throne and there are two sheets left on the roll of toilet paper, it is not time to fill it up, it is time to get even.

I have a total of eighty-four years of experience, adding up two kids and a husband at an average of twenty years each and three dogs at an average of eight years.

Clearly, I am overqualified for most available jobs that are offered to people without a college degree. On the other hand, I don't have the stomach for a slice of the corporate world. I am not even capable to get through to a live Telus person without losing my cool.

In hindsight, I realize that it was this threatening premonition of emptiness that brought about my resolution. Then again, it might have been fate.

I was into my third year as a dog walker for the local SPCA, when I met Vanessa. She was the most depressed creature I had ever seen dropped off. For three weeks, the frightened "Heinz 57," mother of three, refused to leave the square and bare kennel for even a walk or a pee. The black and white, tailless, shaggy animal just passively vegetated on the concrete floor. Let's face it, these dogs sit on death row and on this specific day, Vanessa was virtually given her last meal. Two pleadingly big brown eyes begged me, shone right into my soul. She needed me.

"I have a surprise for you when you get home," I later called my husband.

"Let me guess, it is SPCA-day. I hope you found the perfect little dog: mature, spayed, short-haired, and well trained?"

"Well, she has beautiful eyes!"

Oliver greeted me: "Out of *all* the dogs passing through at the SPCA, did you *have* to pick this hideous four—legger?" And then smirked: "It is said that a dog resembles its owner!"

Even an ugly dog deserves a nice name. So I renamed her Ally, after the hottest TV character airing at the end of the old and the beginning of the new century: Ally McBeal.

Ally is truly a frightened, disturbed, and needy little thing. It took her several weeks to poke up her ears, open her mouth, and let the tongue hang out. Ally is progressing three steps forward and two steps back. Thanks to my wealth of experience, I am qualified to deal with it.

And maybe one day, I'll write about it.

First published in *The Province*

LOST

WILLY HONKED THE horn of our Jetta.

"Coming!" I yelled, stuffing the last items into my bag and bolting down the stairs, three steps at a time.

"Goodness me! What happened that we have to rush out in such a hurry with muscle-relaxation cream no less?" I asked, securing the seat belt, placing my bag between my legs.

Willy was backing out of our driveway. "The first thing Hermann said was, 'Don't worry. Jeanette and I, we're all right.'"

"What's that supposed to mean?"

While we drove the thirty minutes from town to Dür's cozy vacation home on the shore of Spokin Lake, Willy filled me in. Apparently, our Swiss friends had spent last night stranded in their rented Pontiac near Moffat Lake. Now they had asked Willy's assistance to get the car back.

So many questions went through our heads. Why did they spend a night in the car? If the Pontiac was at Moffat Lake, how did they get back? Jeanette was sixty-seven years old, her husband ten years older still and on heart medication. For the last few times, their yearly journey from Switzerland to Canada had only been manageable by taking several short flights and making overnight stops in Toronto and Vancouver.

Willy manoeuvred our car down the fir-tree lined lane and stopped in front of the cabin. Two weary looking seniors greeted us with gentle but heartfelt hugs and invited us inside. Jeanette was pale, her aristocratic white hair in disarray while Hermann moved slowly, his back hunched. For the first time, the distinguished retirees looked their age.

It was May 27, 2002, five o'clock in the evening. The burning and crackling logs in the wood stove permeated comforting warmth as we all sat down at the small dining room table.

"Yesterday," Jeanette started, "we decided to drive to Ten-ee-ah Lodge at Spout Lake."

They had headed out after lunch and expected to complete the round-trip of 150 km, including the break for an early dinner at the picturesque restaurant, before dark.

Lifting her glass of water, Jeanette said, "A last check on our detailed map offered deceptive reassurance." She took a sip and added, "In hindsight it is unbelievable, why we did not—besides two water bottles and two buns—include our otherwise standard precautionary supplies: blankets, pillows, compass, and extra water."

She then described the carefree beginning of their outing, the grouse and deer sightings and the hope, as always, to see a magnificent black bear. Thirty-five minutes into their excursion, Hermann turned from the gravelled Spokin Lake Road, steering the Pontiac south along the 108 Mile Road. For an-hour-and-a-half they cruised comfortably through the beautiful forests, further and further, believing to follow the road to Spout Lake. Frequently, Hermann stopped the car so they could admire the fantastic scenery and breathe in the scent of evergreens and forage. Once they even filmed a not-so-shy snow rabbit.

"We wondered," Hermann said in a hoarse voice, "why we hadn't encountered any other vehicles since the turn off from Spokin Lake Road. Then again, I reasoned it was not so unusual in this vast country."

The road narrowed and the bends increased. Now there were patches of snow and the terrain became more mountainous. Hermann felt the ground getting soft under the wheels.

He cleared his throat. "Nothing matched the memories of earlier drives to Ten-ee-ah. We decided to be safe and to turn the Pontiac around."

As soon as he came to a stop, the front wheels sank into the ground. The more he tried to get the car out of the mud, the more the tires spun, digging into the mire.

Jeanette tried to laugh, "An obvious Canadian landscape of spring breakup, right?"

Hermann continued, "We dragged kilos of rocks and twigs to the vehicle and attempted to push them under the sunken wheels." He shrugged his shoulders and threw up his hands, "To no avail. After two hours of hard labour, we gave up."

Willy checked his watch. "We better head out. The guy with the tow truck is meeting us shortly."

Hermann profusely apologized for inconveniencing us and explained that he was simply too exhausted to accompany us. He did, however, show us his video footage of their pilgrimage and point on his map to the road that he believed they had drifted onto.

While driving to the 108 junction, we wondered, how Hermann and Jeanette guessed their way back to civilization and how they kept up their strength without food and hardly any water. According to Hermann, they walked, taking only three short breaks, for more than nine hours.

Gordon from the Horsefly Esso Station, had come twenty-five kilometers west and was already waiting for us at the end of Spokin Lake Road. We parked the Jetta and climbed into the truck's cab. It smelled of diesel. The seats were torn, tools, and rags lay scattered on the rubber mat. Truck and driver looked as if they both had a full days work behind them and were ready for a wash. However, Gordon didn't seem to mind giving up his evening. When we offered the details about Moffat Lake, he smiled broadly. "We're in for a long and bumpy ride, folks."

Every few minutes we passed small roads that forked off to God-knows-where. No wonder Hermann and Jeanette got lost. We stayed left, heading east.

With the suspension of the truck nonexistent, I had to hold onto the door handle on my right and to Willy's arm on my left. The driver and Willy tried to carry on a conversation, but the truck made such a racket, it was hard to hear a word that was said.

Each bend presented new scenery, a distant, deep-blue lake, coniferous forest, a precarious bridge, a wide clearing with low bush and wetland. Gordon drove fast and the truck flew over the potholes.

We stopped, opened the door to read the tracks. Two sets of dainty foot prints, revealing people had been dressed for dinner, pointed in the opposite direction. We continued, reached another fork. Any minute, any turn, we expected to see the blue rental car.

Gordon said something to Willy.

I nudged him, "What did he say?"

"'S' grizzly country up here, that's fo'sure," he yelled in my ear.

We drove for another few minutes and stopped again. No mistaking, the distinctive prints were clearly visible in the soft earth. Forging ahead, we reached the elevation where patches of snow clung to the ground on either side of the road. The potholes became deeper, the road narrower. The bush's beauty and wonder turned mysterious and with it, the tension inside the cab intensified.

All of a sudden, there it was, a soiled monument in the middle of the dirt path. We got out and walked around the abandoned car. The front wheels looked as if they were cemented into the ground. The Pontiac was caked with white, dry mud and the front bumper was dented. On the dashboard inside, we saw a note, where Hermann had written the date, time, and direction they were going to head out.

Gordon slipped on his heavy-duty work-gloves. "Good thing I'm here, no bloody way you'd get this babe out," he said and got busy with chains and hooks. Gently and patiently he wiggled the car out.

Willy and I kicked the wheels with our boots, braking off the hard dried dirt around the tires. Even the mud-smeared doors were hard to open. The engine, thank heaven, started on the first attempt.

While driving back, Willy, keeping an eye on the odometer, watching as kilometers added up, was visibly shaken. He had met Mr. and Mrs. Dür ten years earlier, when they asked him to look after their holiday retreat during their absences. They had first travelled to Canada in 1967, when Hermann had represented Switzerland at the Summer Olympic Games in Montreal as an equestrian. Further travels led them west, to British Columbia, where they'd purchased the property and the cabin.

Willy and Hermann, both former military men from the old country, connected immediately. Jeanette, an artist and avid environmentalist, fascinated me with her knowledge of every plant and every berry they found on their acreage. She enriched our dinner conversations with stories of bats nesting under their roof or bald eagles fishing in Spokin Lake, and, one year, a black bear prowling around their cabin.

The Swiss vacationers were not ignorant about the Canadian wilderness. As security measure, they always let Willy know of their whereabouts.

Thus, Willy had been aware of their plans to dine at Ten-ee-ah Lodge the night before. Most likely, Willy would have tried to touch base with our friends tonight—had not Hermann made contact first—and become alarmed if nobody had answered the phone. Still with no clue as to where they had picked the wrong turn, it might have taken days to find them. It happens every year in the mountains and forests of British

Columbia and other parts of North America. People get lost. Some are never found.

We timed more than thirty kilometers to the junction where our car was parked. Gordon could have charged a fortune on overtime and extra gas, but he was content with accepting some moderate payment. Then, the Good Samaritan and his coarse truck left, northeast, toward Horsefly.

I drove the Jetta, while Willy chauffeured the Pontiac back to Dür's lodge, where we arrived after nine o'clock.

Too fatigued to sleep, Hermann and Jeanette were still up, resting in the living room. We moved two dining-room chairs close to the stove and sat down, inhaling the aroma of ointment and burning wood. Jeanette served us tea and told us the rest of the story.

"By late afternoon, we realized that we were stuck. We would have to spend the night inside the safety of the car." Placing the tea-pot on the stove, Jeanette returned to her rocking chair, nestled into it and threw a blanket over her legs. "To think of relaxing sleep was absurd. It was freezing and my body trembled, not only from the cold. My moral was at an all-time low. Hermann, on the other hand, fought to keep a positive attitude."

The urge to find out their exact location compelled Jeanette outside again.

With a warm look toward her husband, she said, "Hermann cautioned, "Don't you get lost now. Don't leave me."

Hermann, curled up on the couch as if he was not going to ever get up from that soft cushioned seat, smiled at his wife.

Promising to be careful, Jeanette followed the muddy road in front of the broken-down car. As she walked around the first bend, she looked upon a wonderful wilderness lake. She plowed through the ankle-high snow, hoping to see any kind of dwelling along the shore.

"There was nothing," she said, gently rocking. "Along the way I had found wolf, moose, and bear prints. Here, at the lake, I saw forest, forest, and more forest. When I plodded back toward the road, I came upon a dangling sign on a fir tree; faded letters spelled 'Moffat Lake'."

Back at the car, they found Moffat Lake on their map and realized, they had erred far to the east.

"An increasing will to prevail stirred inside me," Jeanette continued, "Crystal clear, I remembered some fundamental survival rules: sleep and rest is number one. I found some sedatives in my purse and we both took one. They did calm me and alleviated my anxiety."

In a clear voice, Hermann said, "I swallowed the emergency supply of my heart medication."

Hearing his accurate words surprised me for I suspected he had given into his exhaustion and was asleep. Now though, finished talking, he closed his eyes.

Jeanette continued telling us that for the following hours inside the Pontiac, they drifted in and out of sleep. At five o'clock in the morning with stiff, cold feet, the old Swiss couple started the most uncertain march of their lives.

They stuffed the small bottles with clean snow and placed them inside their pockets, packed video, binocular, emergency kit, the map, an umbrellas, and pepper spray. Carefully, they studied the tracks of their car in order to follow them back. The last thing they wanted was getting lost in a new direction.

"Approximately one hundred metres away from our destitute car," Jeanette said, "we discovered, in the morning frost the first steam-fresh bear droppings. From my studies, I strongly suspected that I was looking at grizzly bear faeces. I urged Hermann to speed up our pace."

To save energy, they didn't talk much. But they did discuss the possibility of not making it out alive.

Hearing this, Willy and I exchanged looks.

"I didn't want to die," Jeanette said, readjusting her blanket.

After three hours of steady walking, they allowed themselves a break and a small, very small, sip of water. Hermann laid down on some soft moss, where they think he picked up the tick they found on him earlier tonight.

Ten minutes later, they kept on moving. Along the way, they found more animal droppings: coyotes', fox's, wolves', as well as more bear's, and possibly a cougar's.

The naturalist said, "More than the dubious feeling of being unarmed, the question why so many predators relieve themselves in the middle of a road arose."

Before I could question her unexpected train of thought, she explained, "I was thankful, to have something else to worry about and came, after some brooding, to this conclusion: for many animals, excrements are territorial markings. Where better visible than on a road?"

"Words from a true ecologist," I laughed.

After nine-and-a-half hours of marching that turned into trudging and finally almost crawling, they reached the fork, where they had chosen the wrong path the previous day.

Hermann, who sat with his hands resting on his lap as if praying, opened his eyes and, obviously having followed his wife's story telling, said, "I collapsed into the ditch and knew that I could not take another step."

Jeanette told us, she placed the opened umbrella so to shade her worn out husband. "At dawn," she continued, "we had fought the cold and now the afternoon sun scorched relentlessly upon us. My tongue stuck to my dry palate. In front of my eyes stars were dancing." Tears welled in her eyes when she finished, "Then our angel came."

Viktor, who was on his way from Horsefly to 108 Mile House, drove toward the junction. Finding the couple in the middle of nowhere with no car in sight, the local rancher stopped his pickup truck, got out, and asked if they needed help. Jeanette said she felt like kissing the man. Without hesitating, Viktor assisted the exhausted elders into the front seat of his truck. He postponed whatever business he was attending and drove them forty kilometers out of his way, to their cabin.

As any good Swiss citizen would, Hermann pulled his wallet from his back-pocket and asked Viktor how much payment he expected. The rancher waved his hands and replied that surely they would have done the same for him. He accepted a cup of tea and a cookie. Then he left. This, Hermann and Jeanette understood, was the Canadian way.

When we told the survivors-against-many-odds that they had walked for twenty-nine kilometers they didn't seem surprised. Jeanette had already found her humour again.

"I was never so glad *not* to see a bear," she laughed.

For the short two days, their remaining Canadian holiday time, Hermann didn't drive. But our friends did venture for extensive walks in order to prevent their stressed legs from stiffening too badly. The joint-and-muscle cream I had brought was used up by the time Dür's boarded the airplane to return to Switzerland.

Hermann and Jeanette returned to Canada for a rare, second holiday the same year.

They bought a satellite phone.

A Slice of History

ON TOP OF my computer stands a copper bust of Napoleon Bonaparte. Not every person can leave a mark in history as he did. However, some of us are fortunate to be touched by a slice of the past in a personal way—if we take the time to listen.

A kaleidoscope of Rotarians and spouses moved and mingled in the lobby of the Terrace Convention Centre in Northern British Columbia. I waited, trying not to look too lost, for my husband had wandered off to get me a drink.

"Hello. My name is Esio. Esio Marzotto." His words sounded like an Italian opera.

I shook the man's offered hand and looked into a pair of trusting, warm eyes. "Pleased to meet you," I said. "Your name sounds interesting, I have never heard it."

"It's a long story. Maybe later I'll tell you all about it."

Appreciative to have someone to talk to, I wasn't going to let him slip away. "How about right now? I'm curious."

The smell of cooked meat and spicy sauce tantalized our taste buds as everybody waited for the dinner-announcement, to move into the dining area and to be seated for the final dinner at the District Conference of 2002.

Esio looked from his empty wine glass to the lineup at the bar and, deciding to keep me company, he began to speak about his father, Roberto Marzotto.

Roberto was only seventeen years old, when he joined the Italian army. Obviously, his parents were distressed about their youngest son's decision. But the boy left his eleven siblings, parents, and home in Pordenone, Northern Italy, to fight in the First World War. He was assigned to the cavalry division of Captain Esio Babini.

"What are you doing here? You're much too young to fight a war," said the Captain.

"I'm here to honor my country," answered Roberto eagerly.

At this point, a slight shiver ran up my spine. I knew what was coming. I knew the story. I knew the ending. But I was captured by Esio's melodic voice and craved to hear the tale in his own words.

Captain Babini appointed Roberto as his valet and stationed the teenaged soldier close to the commander's tent. Roberto shined the captain's shoes, prepared his meals, and tended to his horse. For months, he fulfilled his duties and hoped to be ordered to the front—into action.

During the last autumn days in 1918, the cavalry broke camp and moved to the shore of the Tagliamento River, near Venice. The next few days would become notable and brilliant accomplishments for the Italians. Heavy fighting took place and the havoc years to ameliorate.

With the help of my new friend, the raconteur's vivid description, I saw a foggy morning and imagined smelling wet earth, mixed with gunpowder and horses. My mind created a scene of anxious soldiers mounting their animals and assembling without much talking. I heard nervous hoof-steps, rifles banging against halters, and felt the tension in the air as I continued listening to Esio.

Roberto grabbed his gun, ready to fight for his country. But to his great discontent, Captain Babini refused Roberto's wish to march into combat.

"You, son, stay here and be ready when we return."

It was an order.

"Here you are!" My husband intruded.

I pressed my lips together and took his hand. He understood my gesture, nodded toward Esio and listened to the tale end of his narration.

At the shore of the Tagliamento, the Italians fought against the German-Austrian forces. It was one of the last battles of World War I. Many lost their lives. The wounded crept and hobbled back in confused horror. Roberto waited in vain. Captain Esio Babini lost his life that morning.

Like so many young men, Roberto returned home with internal scars that only fellow soldiers can fathom. He eventually married and immigrated to Toronto where his first child was born. To honor the man who had protected Roberto as a father would his son, Roberto named his firstborn child Esio.

My hands were shaking. I tried to say something, thank him for sharing this piece of his family-history, but there was a lump in my throat. The crowd at the Terrace Arena started to move toward the dining hall.

With a wave and a smile Esio said, "Enjoy your dinner," and joined his group of table companions.

For weeks, the story haunted me. I asked myself why this man's past had made such an impact on me? Was it the name? The man? The story?

It was all that and more. Every family has a past, every person a story. If not us, who will pass them on? We, each of us, are a slice of history. Our forefathers' lives branded and shaped us. Because of our family's past—or in spite of it—we are who and where we are today.

Esio gave me permission to write his story and admitted, "I wished I had asked more details, but my dad did not talk much about the war."

Captain Babini was as great a man to Roberto Marzottos' family as Napoleon was to the French. Somewhere, at least, Captain Esio Babini deserves to be written about.

First published in *Canadian Stories*

WHAT GOES AROUND COMES AROUND

WHEN MY HUSBAND, Willy, and I decided to leave Switzerland twenty-four years ago, we anticipated excitement and encouragement from our parents. Instead we got tears and trepidations: "What do you think is better over there?" "What about the family business?" "When are you coming back?"

In Canada, we lived the "Eurodream" and became landowners. We stood on our property in rural British Columbia—with no hookup to electricity or water—and proudly hugged the trees that we called ours. Then we chopped them down for a better view. We bought a ladder, climbed onto the roof of our trailer, and sat for hours. From our perch we saw only trees, hills, and the Coast Mountains. We listened to the silence.

To our parents we wrote: "There is so much space here. We can build anything we want on our property without applying for a permit. We can hang our laundry on the line outside on Sunday and no neighbour will complain. We can get hired by just showing up for work. At night, we can see the stars."

Our families made bets on how long we would last.

By the time our first child, Oliver, was born, we still collected the rainwater off the roof. The diapers I washed in a canning pot on the wood stove.

One Saturday morning, when we were building yet another addition to our trailer, our neighbours showed up, hammers in hand, for a work bee. One of the wives came along and explained to me that it was my job to feed everybody. Frantically, I ran from storage room to freezer and started to get busy in the kitchen. By dinner time the roof was up. With the smells of freshly baked bread and barley-soup melding in with the scent of sawdust and sweat, we sat and laughed around the kitchen table late into the night.

Our moms could not believe that people volunteered without getting paid.

We wrote to our parents that Canadian forests are so vast, people get lost in them every year. We mailed pictures of a black bear that had climbed one of the trees still standing in our front yard.

Back in Switzerland, they called us "braggers."

When Oliver was two, our daughter, Melanie, was born and we had a dog—and running water.

One by one, groups of our relatives and friends trickled in for a few weeks at a time. We put our children through a crash course in Swiss German and promised them Ninja Turtles, if they made an effort to communicate. We drove six hundred kilometers to Vancouver to pick up our visitors. We toured Barkerville, BC, and took our guests fishing "out west." We barbequed steaks, stacked as high as the Swiss Alps.

When the first of our parents, my husband's father, passed away, the pressure to come home intensified. We wrote to both families that our home was here. Proudly, we announced that we had become Canadian citizens.

The notes of congratulations from our families were halfhearted.

We outgrew our hillbilly life and moved to the small town of Williams Lake. Our little family of four planted some solid roots, with neighbours and friends becoming aunts and uncles. The children sold chocolates for school and played soccer and baseball. Seven years later, we moved into a bigger house.

We spent our summer vacations camping. Oliver and Melanie got a paper route. We saved and drove to Disneyland. The kids played piano and Nintendo. On their sixteenth birthdays, they got their drivers' licenses. All through senior high school we told our son and daughter to turn down the volume of the *Much Music* channel.

For Christmas dinner, however, we still preferred a creamy Cheese Fondue to turkey and mashed potatoes.

Back in Switzerland, our mothers were becoming resigned, "You will never come back, will you?"

Sometimes life has a way of coming full circle. One year after Oliver's graduation, he applied for an Australian visa.

When the response arrived, my husband insisted on delivering it to our son's workplace immediately. Oliver finished twirling the pizza dough, wiped his floured hands on his apron, and ripped open the envelope with a wide grin on his face. We squeezed each other's hands tight, feeling a thousand emotions running through our veins. Oliver yelled, "I'm in!"

My husband nodded at me and whispered, "Remember." He stretched out his hand, "Congratulations, son. We know exactly how you feel—believe me, we do."

I swallowed hard and followed suit.

We are getting good at swallowing: Melanie is awaiting confirmation for student-exchange programs to Germany and Spain.

First published in *Canadian Living*

To See or Not to See

I NEED NEW GLASSES. Fabulous! First of all, my vision will soon improve. Secondly, with the optometrist's new prescription, I have an excuse to purchase new frames, a fresh look.

Since I was two years old, my glasses became—and still are—the last thing I take off at night and the first thing I put on in the morning. My nose and face grew around the frames. Without glasses I feel naked. Without them I am severely vision impaired.

Lately though, even with my spectacles on, I have felt blind. It happened gradually. First, the listed ingredients on packaged items became unreadable and faces on TV foggy. Then, the lines of the morning paper danced uncontrollably. And finally, while driving along a new stretch of highway, I was unable to follow the signs because by the time I could decipher them, it was too late to take that turn.

As excited as I am about a soon-to-be improved vision and a new look, I have a dilemma. How can I possibly decide what frame to choose, when without wearing my glasses, I can't recognize my own face in the mirror?

It is imperative to ask the right person to come along. Would my husband agree to any look simply because he was in a hurry? Or worse, would he glance at the price tag first and give a secondary glance at how the rim complimented my features? Would my writing buddy make sure I look five years her senior? Would my girlfriend talk me into funky, red frames, which I would tire of after two months? I decided to put my trust in my daughter, Melanie.

Having worn glasses since 1958, there are none I haven't seen, tried on, or bought before: frames big and small, round and rectangular, metal and titanium, lenses tinted and clear, generic and high index, and single and—yes—bifocal. I'll never, however, forget the worst pair.

I was in grade four when my parents purchased the most dreadful black frames, shaped like butterfly wings, with rhinestones at the top corners. They bought them because I had stepped on my brand-new glasses and had broken the frames beyond repair. Finances forced my parents to find frames that fit the already cut and shaped lenses. I got teased from here to Timbuktu about those glasses.

By now, my choice is limited for different reasons. The frames can't be big or the strong lenses will sit too heavy on my nose. Nor can they be super small, for then the complicated prescription can't be fitted. My daughter and I quickly narrow the selection to three, and finally agree on a blue frame.

I sign the order form and pay my deposit.

A week later, I anxiously place the new glasses on my nose.

Instantly, my world changes. I can see black irises' in the blue eyes of the sales assistant. I see the buttons on her dress. I see scratches on the counter top. I see a pattern on the carpet.

"I can see! Thank you." Turning toward the mirror I look at, "Mother?"

I look again. Who is this old lady with the wrinkled face? There must be something wrong with this prescription. Something, someone, just slapped fifteen years on my face.

It usually takes me a couple of days to get used to new prescriptions. My head aches, I feel dizzy and, more often than not, I have to go back to the store to refit the frame because they are too tight behind the ears, or squeeze my nose. This time, the problem is purely psychological. Every time I pass by a mirror, I look at my face and want to scream. Since the changeover, I have aged at least a decade or two.

There are deep furrows on my forehead. Fine black hairs and more nasty lines are nestled between my upper lip and my nose. Faint, but ugly brown spots fleck my cheeks. Two deep parentheses frame my mouth.

I call my hairdresser. "This is an emergency," I tell her. "I need highlights, a cut, a young look."

But the blonde streaks and the sporty new style don't restore my skin to that of a thirty-year-old.

It takes a while to accept the new me and warm up to the creases in my face. Less and less I take offence to the result of life's worries permanently engraved in my skin. More and more I see testimony of a fifty-five-year-old, happy woman, for the most profound wrinkles are my laugh lines.

My new look is fabulous.

River Valley Trail

E VER SINCE THE last specks of persistent frozen crystals cried into the ground last spring, I have waited for this—the first snow fall. I am one of these crazy people who love winter. It is November. Promising.

Here, in the Cariboo, the time span between the last and the first frost might be three months—if we're lucky.

I drive along Mackenzie Avenue and turn into Soda Creek road, leaving the buzz of Williams Lake's industrial area and sawmills behind me. The parking lot "past the dump"—that's how we call the location because that's where the city's refuse is located—is empty. I feel frivolous to be the first arriving at the seven kilometer mark of the Williams Lake River Valley Trail. To step into the untouched snow is a privilege for which no gilt-embossed invitation is necessary.

With my camera in the pocket of my down-filled winter jacket, I stomp through the snow in my oversized Sorel boots—oversized for extra sock space when the temperature drops to minus twenty degree Celsius or more.

Thousands of years ago, this area was flooded. Now, magnificent sandy cliffs frame the valley, north and south of its corridor.

The trail worms along and over Williams Creek. Douglas-fir and white birch greet me with their, under the burden of heavy snow, crackling branches. A few crows cry just because they like to complain. Crimson rose hips hang stubbornly between the prickly bushes. The gray sky promises more precipitation. Already, I breathe through frozen nose hair.

Pausing on one of the many small bridges, some of which have been constructed from old railway cars, I lean over the wooden railing. The water fights to keep moving in this cold, while dead salmon, overlooked by bears and eagles, decompose in the shallow waters. Winter has neutralized the smell. Soon, layer by thin layer, ice will bring the creek's flow to a trickle.

I continue and now find the odd prints from fox and deer. Camouflaged eyes might be watching me; Pygmy owls and Goshawk are supposed to reside here year-round.

This is my Canada, where I breathe in devoutly the cold, clean air, feel it bite down my throat into my lungs. Here, I listen to nature and, for a moment, forget everything else.

Even though I have lived in Canada for almost thirty years now, I still profoundly appreciate this—our freedom and space.

The valley gets narrower. Snow is unable to stick to the overhangs of the steep sand cliffs. A good hour into my walk, I look up at rock faces where intricate erosion-layered designs are freckled with precariously leaning evergreens, their roots hanging on for dear life. It's like walking through an art gallery.

Descending on a gently slopped trail, I reach the last curve and—the end of the River Valley Trail. Here, approximately five kilometers from the parking lot, Williams Creek joins the Fraser River, salmon's waterway to the Pacific Ocean six hundred kilometers away.

I push through the winter beach. It is snowing now. Dark clouds embrace the trees and the heavy flakes melt into the mighty Fraser. Water slaps over rocks. Nothing stands in the way of the river's destination. I would like to be this focused.

In a couple months, by January, ice boulders, some the size of cars, will have been tossed topsy-turvy on this shore. I will come back—many times—with my camera.

The photos will console me, next summer, when the August heat suffocates me and, once more, I long for the first snow to fall.

First published in *Die Kleine Zeitung mit Herz*

UNIVERSAL LANGUAGE

ENGLISH, SO THE common knowledge went during my growing up in Switzerland, is the universal language. Despite this 1960s educational insight, English didn't become the mandatory foreign language taught until the new millennium.

Before the turn of the century, the second linguistic requirement was either, French, Italian, or German, depending on the Swiss region a student lived in and what their mother tongue was.

My first language was Swiss German. Swiss German dialects were mostly oral communication, seldom written. Therefore, in grade one, we learned to speak and write the proper German—High German. In grade six, I started studying French.

Since neither German, nor French were going to help me in Vancouver, I signed up for a two-week crash-course in London, England, before immigrating to Canada. After my arrival in British Columbia, though, I quickly realized, my time and money had been wasted. There are drastic variations to this universal language.

In Vancouver, you don't ask a "Bobby" for directions. A waiter will raise his eyebrows at you when inquiring to where the "loo" is. In England, "afters" are, as the words implies, ordered and eaten "after" the meal, whereas here, "afters" are dessert. "It's a pity" is less common than, "it's just too bad." Too bad for me—I was back to square one.

But I was used to terminology obstacles. In Switzerland, every village has its own dialect, using different expressions than those of its neighboring town. My husband will eat a "waehe," while I eat the same pie, but call it "flade." His hometown was a mere one-hour drive from where I used to live. Fifty kilometers further, they spoke French.

At my first job at McDonald's in Vancouver, I tried hard to learn "Canadian." Paying particular attention on how people around me spoke, I thought, surely, I could pick up the nuances in articulation and vocabulary. I urged my coworkers and new friends, "please correct me when I make a mistake or pronounce something wrongly."

"Are you kidding," was always the answer. "Don't lose your accent. It's you. It's cute."

I blame them for my present predicament. Only a week ago, when meeting someone, the introduction went like this:

"Hi, I'm Verena, pleased to meet you."

"I'm Surrendor Pooni. So very nice to meet you. Where you from?"

"Williams Lake."

"And before? Before Williams Lake, where you from? Germany perhaps?"

"I am Canadian," I insist, but admit, "I was born in Switzerland."

"Very nice. How long you here?"

At this point, I could have saved my dignity by throwing the question right back. But instead I tried to mumble an unidentifiable, "twenty-four years," and attempted a somewhat graceful exit.

Having lived in Canada now more years than in Switzerland, I am deeply ashamed to speak as if I just stepped off the boat. I am frustrated that I never figured out the British Columbian dialect. Really, what are the Canadian West Coast linguistic characteristics? Had we settled in Newfoundland, I am certain, it would have taken me only a wee-bit of time to adapt to the distinctly recognizable Irish-Scottish variation of English. But throughout this province, the demographics are an assimilation of immigrants from all over the world and the speech is such a diversification of accents that it leaves one with nothing concrete to grab onto.

I turned to media. For a while, I listened intently to the national news, repeated Peter Mansbridge's words like a parrot. I liked his nasal speech, particularly how he put the emphasis on "can" into Canada. For the rest, I didn't hear much difference between Mr. CBC and myself. I was under the happy illusion to be successfully deemphasizing my German-French phonetics. My children disagreed.

During their rebellious teenage years, when they were embarrassed by parents who spoke a little less than perfect, they nagged and corrected us. Typically for kids, they were only interested in vocabulary concerning breaking wind or digestion. "Mom, you don't flash the toilet, you flush the toilet."

Well, technically . . .

As it stands, the best I can do, is raise the tone of every last sentence fragment by half an octave and then finish with "eh?"

I console myself by reading. English literature, after all, can be done silently, accent free. Lately though, some surprising vocabulary integrating has caught my attention. I found in Canadian published novels these German words: Schadenfreude, Zerstreutheit, Eifersucht, verklemmt . . .

On the other hand, when I opened a German book that I recently received from my sister Maegi, I read these English expressions within the first five pages: "Just for fun . . ." "layouts . . ." "gigantic . . ."

This lexis-merger is also evident each time we visit Switzerland. Magazines have pages titled, "Words of wisdom" and "Letter from the editor." Store windows advertise "Discounts" and "Blow-out Sales." And for young people, like my nieces and nephews, things are "mega cool" and "rad." They eat neither "waehe" nor "flade"; they go "fooding" and eat "pie."

I have missed that boat, missed picking up modern slang. I still speak the unspoiled Swiss-German commonly applied three decades ago, when I emigrated. Other than the occasional slip up with sentence structure, my Swiss-German is so pure and antiquated, even my mother occasionally says to me, "That was cute. I haven't heard that word in years."

So Canadians and my mother agree; I am cute. At my age, I don't particularly care to be cute.

Being imperfect now in my mother tongue as well as in English, I see only one hope: The universal language might be evolving back, via Anglo-Saxon, French, Latin to its Germanic origin, ending at a place—in between English, French, and German—the place I am at.

This nascent Esperanto I would call Fermglish and I, and all other immigrants in the same language gridlock as I, would speak it without an accent.

Me, My Cars, and I

CARS ARE IMPORTANT to most people. I learned that thirty years ago when, while introducing my boyfriend, I received eyebrow-lifting nods of approval—not for him—for his car.

Even my boss was impressed, "I like this young man. He drives a Volvo."

So that's what the metallic-green car was; so that's what the "V" on the hood stood for—Volvo. All I knew was that I didn't like the leather seats that felt either cold and slippery or hot and sticky.

For me, a car is nothing more than a means of transportation getting me from A to B. As long as the engine starts when I turn the key, I'm happy. Over the years I have driven different cars, but all I remember about them is their colour—and their temperament.

There was the school bus-coloured VW van. (I remember VW because they are my and my husband's initials.) This van's "tic" was the battery light. When it came on, I had to pull over, get out, squeeze under the front of the car and wiggle a wire. This turned into a real problem when I was seven months pregnant.

We traded the yellow van for a used aqua-blue station—something that stopped running whenever it felt like it. Naturally, this mostly happened on the hottest summer days while my baby and toddler exercised their vocal cords. We then had to push the vehicle to a safe spot and let the car (and kids) cool off.

Five years later, a second-hand sandy-beige van replaced the aqua-blue station-something. The van was a real bargain and was supposed to be perfect for chauffeuring kids to and from school and extracurricular activities. Unfortunately, with its notorious engine failures, its maintenance cost more than mine and the children's combined, including all sports equipment and school-supplies.

We matured to a two-vehicle family and I received an olive-green hand-me-down all to myself. That rust-speckled car earned me the title: "Queen of flat tires" at a local tire store.

Obviously, I was ambivalent about "bonding" with cars. I liked them when I needed them and hated them when they didn't perform. I never gave a car a second thought for I had much more important worries.

Worries such as how to efficiently make my way through the aisles of the grocery store and hopefully pick the quickest-moving line at the cash register. By the time I was done with my shopping, I often had forgotten where I left my means of transportation. Pushing the full buggy, I would circle the parking lot from the outside-in, searching for my car, hoping nobody noticed my incompetence.

One day, as I marched toward the olive-green hand-me-down, I fished the key out of my purse promising my kids dinner at McDonald's, if only they would behave civilized for a few more minutes. I inserted the key, but it wouldn't turn in the lock. While the children started a fist fight around my freshly bought eggs, I wiggled the key out and tried again.

Suddenly, the window was pulled down from the inside and a friendly young woman asked, "Can I help you?"

I did what any mature mother would do; I jumped, threw the keys in the air and screamed.

My life changed drastically though, when we bought my brand-new Honda CRV—The perfect blend of freedom and sporty fun. My CRV has an "Inline four-cylinder engine," is fully loaded with "air-conditioned filtration system," "power-door and tailgate lock," and includes a "five year no-nonsense warranty." From the first day I owned it, I felt the bonding. I breathed in deeply the new vinyl and fabric-scent. I caressed the dashboard. I wanted to name it. I became a regular at the car wash and wiped my dog's paws before allowing her to jump in. I took detours driving home. Me and my car, we fit.

My husband placed two red-and-white stickers, reading "I am Canadian," on each side window so that I would no longer embarrass myself—and him, we live in a small town—by fondling with other people's car locks. But that was not going to be a problem anymore. I had bonded with my Honda—or so I thought.

Last week I parked, grabbed a buggy, rushed inside the grocery store and—as always—worried, how fast I could get my shopping done. Once again I picked the wrong lineup at the cash register. The customer ahead of me wanted this and that price-checked, demanded the groceries boxed, and finally needed a carton of cigarettes, which had to be fetched from a locked cupboard at the other side of the store.

Finally, having done my paying and bagging, I hurriedly pushed my full shopping cart toward the Honda CRV. I took the remote control key out of my jacket pocket and pointed to the back door. Nothing happened. "Could the battery be empty already?" I wondered.

"Just a minute," I heard someone say. "I'll open my car and you can fill it with your groceries."

Dumbfounded I looked at a middle-aged man who laughed, "That is my car." After a moment he added, "Your silver-grey Honda is probably the one over there, the one with the stickers on the windows."

"Thank you," I mumbled, turned my beet-red face and my buggy around and marched in the opposite direction.

I think my next car should be Barbie pink.

First published in *Savvy Women's Magazine*

DESTINATION ANNIVERSARY

For our twenty-fifth anniversary, our children shocked and surprised us with a meticulously planned, booked, and prepaid trip to Barrow. According to the itinerary, we would be at our "end-of-the-world" destination, June 7, 2004.

A couple of days before our departure, Willy searched the Internet and, within minutes, found the Web site of the Assembly of God directory. We e-mailed Pastor David Wilson and his wife Debbie, who were now stationed in Anchorage, and they agreed to meet us for lunch.

We waited, fidgety with anticipation, in the dark, log restaurant that Debbie had suggested. The menus felt sticky and the place smelled of hot oil and fish. In front of us, an enormous stuffed moose head's glassy eyes looked down on us, awakening memories of our visit to Fairbank's Alaskaland park in 1979.

Since our wedding then, I had learned, of course, that Pastor David's way of talking was Texan and his cool "hey man" was an "amen."

When Debbie entered, we recognized her immediately and stood up to greet her.

"How absolutely wonderful to see you." She hugged us. "David and I wondered so often, how you two kids might be doing."

"It's just too bad, he's out of town," Willy said.

"Yes, he would have really liked to see you too." Debbie opened the menu, before she was completely seated. "I suggest the halibut nuggets and corn fritters." She turned to the waitress, "That is what I'll have."

I nodded to Willy and he ordered the same for us. He unzipped our backpack, retrieved our cardboard-laminated, handmade photo album titled, "Today is the first day of the rest of our lives," and pushed it across the table.

Leafing through the few pages of faded wedding pictures, Debbie reminisced, "Oh my, Molly and Noah Itta. Your witnesses. They're still alive, still members of the same church." She unfolded the paper place mat the young waitress in Barrow had signed and given us as her wedding present. "Dora, sweet Dora. Would you believe, she's married now, has four sons and works for Alaska Air?"

Moist-eyed, she returned the album. "I do miss the people," she sighed, "but I don't miss the isolation. There's still no road into Barrow and there probably never will be one," she said. "Everything is still shipped or flown in."

Then Debbie too pulled out photos and showed off her four grandchildren.

Too soon, it was time to say good-bye. For Willy and me, though, our excitement had just begun, as that same afternoon we flew to Fairbanks, and later, boarded the Air Alaska plane to Barrow.

This time all seats were occupied. The passenger beside us introduced himself as Sergeant Mike Donovan. He told us, he had been a police officer in Barrow for twenty-five years.

"Then you must have been there in '79 when we got married," Willy said. "You must really like the cold, to stay in Barrow for so long."

"I got used to the money. The money," he repeated, "is really good."

During the flight, we told Mike about our wedding while he brought us up-to-date on some of the changes. There were three hotels now, more restaurants, even a pizza place and a Chinese restaurant that delivered. The population, of which only about half were native Alaskans, had almost doubled.

"Do you still have trouble with booze?" I asked, reaching to take the stewardess's sandwich and unlatching the table from the seat in front of me.

Mike laughed, "Are you referring to the shooting incident? That sure scared tourists away for a while." Getting lost in thought, there was a short silence and then he continued,"But since then Barrow has graduated from a dry town to a damp town."

"Damp town?" I asked, searching for the end of the sandwich's cellophane wrapping.

"It means, the alcohol restrictions are lifted somewhat. People can bring their own alcohol into town, but only for self-consumption. It is still illegal to sell it."

Willy got back into the conversation, "That guy, who shot the couple, did he ever get caught?"

"Yes he did," Mike said. "As a matter of fact, he's still behind bars."

"I guess you don't have to worry about inmates escaping," Willy grinned. "Where would they run off to?"

"You'd think that, wouldn't you?" Mike also unwrapped his snack. "But we did have an escapee. We decided not to go after him and promptly, the following day he returned, told us how stupid he had been and asked for his bed back."

We accepted the coffees that were served. Holding the Styrofoam cup with both hands, I turned and looked out the window, down at the endless snow and ice-covered tundra. From the seats behind us, I overheard passengers carrying on a lively discussion about stars and telescopes. *Probably government employees returning to their well-paid research or government jobs.* Finishing my coffee, I leaned back and closed my eyes.

I woke to the pilot's announcement that we were descending for landing. Tables were folded up, seats pushed into position as the plane circled over the Beaufort and Chukchi Sea that shone in brilliant blue against the white shore.

A few minutes later, we stepped through the new airport building's glass-sliding-doors. We rolled our two suitcases across the packed dirt road that was remarkably drier than last time, and entered the King Eider Hotel. Even though the inn looked brand-new, they must have been through one or two muddy spring-seasons, as the check-in girl asked us to remove and leave our shoes in the lobby. We signed the guest book, confirming our children's reservation for two nights.

In our room, Willy slumped onto the queen-sized bed and unfolded the hotel's brochure that had been placed on the comforter. He piled up both pillows, rested his head on them, and read aloud, "Barrow. A bird watcher's Mecca."

"Really?" I asked, opening the window. Breathing in the pure cold air, I heard Willy's pamphlet recitation: "King Eider was one of thousands of migratory birds and ducks that returned each year to nest and breed here during June and July."

Poking my head out further, I listened for the cry of seagulls or quacking of ducks, but didn't hear or see any birds. I noticed, in an unrefined humble backyard across from the hotel, two Huskies lazing in the sun and beside what appeared to be an abandoned home, an American flag fluttering from a wooden, white-painted pole.

The next morning we strolled, dressed in winter clothes, hand in hand through the streets in the direction of the Assembly of God church, where the Sunday service was to begin in half an hour. The weary exterior of the houses along the way looked the same as twenty-five years ago.

The sun shone strongly into our faces, as if stretching out its rays in welcome. By August, we had read, this relentless sun will extract vegetation from the firmly frozen ground, but this was June and as of yet, not one blade of new grass had managed to push through the grey earth.

We entered the church and followed the other parishioners into the main section of the building. I gasped at the rich red carpeted pulpit and the finely finished wooden altar that were in such sharp contrast to the window-less room we hat gotten married in.

Trying to decide which pew to slide into, Willy and I noticed an old man sitting by himself. We squeezed by him and sat down.

Willy looked at him closer. "Noah?" He whispered to me, turned, and tapped him on the shoulder.

"Hello Noah. Do you remember us?"

At first the old man with the still almost black, full hair, looked puzzled. Then his eyes sparkled and he grabbed Willy's hand, grinning so hard, his whole upper body shook.

He jumped to his feet with such vigor that he needed to hold onto the back of the bench to regain his balance. "I have to go home and tell Molly," he said, and, once steadied, hurried out of the church.

After the sermon, we looked for Noah and Molly, but could not see them, or anybody else we recognized. We went to "Pepe's" Mexican Restaurant. The owner, as flamboyant a character as her sombreros on the walls, asked us to sign her guest book, and gave us, because we visited Barrow once and returned, free postcards.

Our digestion-walk led us to the beach. The ice had broken away from the sandy shore exposing small patches of water. We were unable to see beyond the mounds of craggy ice further out. Waves had washed the beach into layers of fine sifted sand, gravel and polished, robin-egg sized pebbles. I pushed my shoes into it, wanting sand to seep into my socks, wanting to feel, if not mud on my shoes, then at least some sort of earthy substance, to take me back to 1979. Except for the blue sky, the still scenery, the seascape was a palette of beige and grey. It smelled of nothing, it smelled white. Yet the picture before us touched my heart more tenderly than the most exotic orchid garden ever could.

"Hey! Are you the anniversary couple?"

Willy smiled, putting his arm around me. "Yes, we are." To me he said, "The word is out."

"Actually, we overheard you talking on the plane," one said. "I'm Richard," and pointing to his friends, he introduced, "Jeff, Scott, and David. We're astronomers," he explained. "Well," he corrected, "amateur astronomers. We've come to Barrow to watch the transits of Venus across the solar disk, tomorrow night."

"Hmmm. That's nice." I didn't have a clue what he just said.

Ignoring our nonenthusiasm, Jeff broke in, "It's a big deal. People from all over the world are flying in to witness it. We will be able to see it here, because the sun doesn't set."

"As long as the weather holds," one interrupted.

"Oh yeah?" Willy said.

The others nodded, eagerly.

Scott, or was it David, continued, "The last time this phenomenon occurred was 125 years ago. As of today, no living man has seen it."

"Wow," we both said, still taking all this information in halfheartedly.

They continued telling us passionately how they found the perfect spot, west of town, behind the airport, to set up their equipment.

Richard finished, "We were thinking—since Venus is the goddess of love—and this is your anniversary, you might like to come and join us, tomorrow night?"

Kool-Aid and Caribou Stew, Part II

AFTER BREAKFAST ON our anniversary day, June 7, we returned to the airport in search of Dora, the waitress who had given us the signed paper-placemat. As soon as we walked into the main building, we spotted her behind the check-in counter. Dora looked the same, maybe a bit heftier.

While she stood with her eyes fixed on the computer screen, we, eagerly smiling, approached her. Willy said, "Hello. You probably don't remember us . . ."

She looked up, then from Willy to me, back to Willy and me again, and squealed, pointing at me, "I have a picture of your wedding."

We laughed and hugged and laughed and hugged some more. Then we asked her if she could help us find Noah and Molly Itta.

Reaching for the phone receiver, she said, "Let me phone them first. You can't just drop in."

She made several calls. Her guttural Native speech, sounding to us like clacking, blithe chatter, was impossible to understand or guess what the topic of conversation was. Finally, she hung up the phone, wrote something on a piece of paper and handed it to Willy.

"Here's the address," she said, "Noah and Molly invited you over to their house. That's a big honor." She lifted her right hand, "Listen," she waved her index finger, "Go straight over there right now and stay as long as they want you to. They're our elders and we respect them. Now, go," she dismissed us, "and let me get back to work. Look for me tonight down at the beach; we're having a huge celebration."

Minutes later, we stood in front of the house. The Inupiat couple opened the door before we had a chance to knock. Compared to Noah's wrinkled face, Molly's velvety, tanned skin looked young, forties young. Her sincere eyes compelled me to bend down and kiss her in the French fashion, on each cheek. She chuckled.

"Thank you for inviting us to your home," Willy said as we entered and removed our shoes. The warm house smelled of fish and curing.

Noah directed us into the living room, gestured us to sit on two fire-red, vinyl-covered kitchen chairs. Mine felt a bit unstable. Our hosts sank into the sofa, their shrunken bodies almost being eaten up by the flower-patterned, soft pillows. For a few awkward moments we sat smiling at each other across the bright room, separated only by a bare coffee table. I was hot and felt like a rare flower being displayed on a pedestal inside a greenhouse. Finally, Willy started a choppy conversation. Our wedding witnesses' slurred English was hard to understand.

We did, however, learn that ten years ago, Noah had survived cancer. Counting on her arthritic fingers, Molly listed the names of her children. She spoke very softly, but I understood when she said, "I think I'm missing one." Willy asked how many grandchildren they had. Both laughed and simply answered, "Many." Then they pointed to the wall of framed and unframed photos some hanging and some thumb-tacked onto the wall behind them.

I stood up and handed them the gifts we had brought: copies of our wedding pictures, photos of our children, and a book of the Cariboo.

Their thank-you was a nod, almost a bow. Noah said, "Now, we give you something."

"You don't have to give us anything," Willy replied, embarrassed. "We came to thank you again for standing up at our wedding."

Noah simpered, "And the love is still in the air."

He pushed himself to the edge of the couch, rocked back and forth until he had the momentum to rise and stand up. Then he scanned their sparsely furnished room.

Willy and I looked at each other. *What could they possibly give us?*

Following a short dialogue between Molly and Noah, he unhooked something from the wall. At each end of two twisted strings hung a furball. Pointing to them, Noah explained, "polar bear."

I gaped, grabbed for Willy's hand and repeated, "polar bear?"

Nodding, Noah smiled and showed us the knob connecting the cords. His eyes sparkled when he said, "polar bear tooth."

"Willy" I whispered, "this is incredible."

Noah stepped toward the hallway, looked at us, smiled, and began to swing one cord while holding onto the other. Suddenly, he sped up, directing one string in one direction while letting go of the other, circling it in the opposite direction. It looked easy enough. But when I tried it, Molly and Noah doubled over with laughter at my clumsy, unsuccessful attempts.

Willy's voice was shaky when he said, "We will always treasure your gift to us."

Molly stood up. It was our cue to leave.

Outside, the afternoon sun was high and the wind fierce, as we traipsed along a dirt road between the village and a lagoon. Along the fresh water's edge was a strip of beige beaten down foliage that looked like last year's forgotten, by snow and cold, squashed hay.

Letting go of my hand, Willy ran into the middle of an intersection. "All traffic halt!" he bantered.

"What?" I laughed. Then I saw what Willy joked about, pulled the camera from my pocket and took a picture of the oh-so-redundant stop sign.

Further along the road, we came to a new arena. As we strolled by the front entrance, the doors opened with a bang and several school-aged children stormed out. Shouting and screaming, they grabbed their bicycles from the rack and raced each other down the road. Many wore only T-shirts and shorts. It made me shiver.

Around the corner was a store and we entered, partly to warm-up, partly to browse. Within the tiny space, one could buy anything from light bulbs, paint, camping supplies, windshield-wipers, to condoms, and fresh bananas. Despite the horrendous prices, we purchased a package of Kool-Aid and a blister pack of trail-mix.

Munching the nuts and raisins we continued, marching now to keep us warm. Eventually, we looped back, arriving at the beach again. We heard voices and before long, we joined a parade of villagers heading toward the shore. They all carried Tupperware containers or Ziplock bags. A couple of the women looked, at first glance, hunchbacked, but then I saw babies' heads sticking out from their parkas. Not two of these gaily decorated parkas looked the same. Near the water, there was a pickup truck with an open tailgate. Inside the box stood huge, round, stainless-steel pots. And on the side frame sat Dora, ladle in hand.

Without warning, the mingling stopped and people gathered around the tailgate. The men removed their caps; everybody bowed their heads. Someone began to chant. My eyes followed the sound and found an old man, hands folded, praying.

"Amen" he said.

The crowd echoed "Amen" and began to move toward Dora, forming a line in front of the pots. One by one, they stretched out their containers, and one by one, they received a scoop of stew. Some ate it right there, others carried their sealed cups or bags away. One lady offered us her full plastic container. "Take it. I already had some."

"Thank you," I said, surprised. Recognizing the meaty aroma from our wedding, I knew it was caribou stew.

Dora waved us over. "Come," she yelled, jumping from the truck, "I want you to meet my Dad." Putting her arm around the shoulders of the man who had led the prayer, she said in a formal, proud tone, "May I introduce Arnold Brower, senior whaling captain, eighty-nine years young." She kissed him on the cheek. "My Dad was the president of the International Whaling Commission and played a vital role in preserving the right for us to hunt bowhead whales."

We shook hands. "Pleased to meet you."

"My dad's clan caught a whale earlier this year," Dora explained, beaming at her father. "And now we're feeding the whole town."

"So this," I asked, perplexed, waving the plastic cup, "is whale stew?"

"No," Dora laughed, "the whale was cut up and shared right away. Today we're serving caribou stew and goose soup." She handed her ladle to a teenaged boy. "My son," she said as he climbed onto the box of the truck. We moved to the side, making room for more families to be served.

Willy asked Arnold, "How many whales do you bring in?"

Arnold lifted his hand, "Just a moment," and turned his attention to a cluster of young and old Inupiat who waited to talk to him.

"I hope," Dora answered for her father, "you're not one of those environmentalists, those radicals who oppose our hunting?"

"Not at all," Willy said. "I used to make my living butchering animals myself. I'm curious though, how old do these whales get?"

This time it was Arnold who replied, in perfect English, "Sometimes we find spear heads in bowhead whales that were used for hunting more than a hundred years ago." Nodding, he let us process this information and then said, "You tell me how old those whales get." His eyes wandered, scanning the scene around him, and we understood that our chat was over.

Dora and her Dad resumed mingling, and we made our way to another group of villagers further down by the beach. About twenty Inupiat people, most of them with their fur-trimmed parka-hoods pulled up over their black hair, stood in a circle. Each of them held onto a twine-loop that was attached to a large, round, dried hide, almost the size of Noah and Mollie's living room. A youngster stepped onto the skin. Chanting and cheering, the carriers pulled and taunted the hide, tossing the jumper in the air, so high, I could see the bottom soles of his moccasins. As we stood and watched, the wind stabbed through my jacket and sweater.

"I'm freezing cold," I whined, "Can we go back to the hotel?"

In our room we sat at the small table and shared our little picnic dinner. Savoring every bite of the caribou stew and toasting with the strawberry-flavoured Kool-Aid, we mused over the buffet Pastor Wilson and his wife had served us in 1979.

It was almost ten o'clock by the time we went looking for the astronomers. Wearing all the clothes I could possibly layer on, we walked to the end of the airport runway. Similar to the lagoon's edge, the flatland here was grassy and the ground spongy. Clouds had moved in. By the time, we joined Richard, Jeff, David, Scott, and others who had all sorts of telescopic equipment set-up in the field, they told us we had missed the first sighting. Placing the lid on the telescope lens, Richard consoled us, "There's a good chance the sky will clear again. We hope."

One of the other astronomers readjusted his instrument, pointing it lower and further west toward the open water. "In the meantime, come and take a look at this," he invited us.

Following his verbal instructions, I focused the lenses and at first, made out only marsh, but then spotted dark rocks—rocks that moved. "Wow." I said recognizing the rocks as birds, "There must be hundreds of them."

Willy said, "Let me see," and I stepped aside.

"More like thousands of birds," he marveled.

"They're migrating ducks," the owner of the telescope explained.

"The colours on some of them are incredible," Willy said, "orange, black, and white."

Richard joined the conversation, "King Eider."

"King Eider," I repeated, anxious to take another probe.

Amongst more people arriving was a reporter, microphone and recorder in hand. Even the town judge made an appearance. A crowd of college students jumped out of the back of a pickup truck and grouped around us. The owner of the Utility Maintenance Building, on whose property we stood, served coffee. One Inupiat woman brought a plastic bag full of pop cans. Another offered us, from a Cool-Whip container, warm, bite-sized black-and-white, "muktuk," whale skin and blubber. Willy took a piece and brought it to my mouth, the same way he had fed me a bite of Debbie's wedding cake.

"For the next twenty-five years," he said.

The skin was a bit rubbery to chew, but the overall taste was unexpectedly agreeable, similar to lightly salted bacon.

The sky cleared, and the amateur astronomers all hurried back to their instruments.

"There it is," one cried, "you can clearly see Venus." He literally pulled Willy to his scope.

"Is that it?" Willy asked."That tiny little dot in front of the sun is Venus?"

"Isn't she a beauty?" Richard proclaimed. "We're witnessing history folks."

All of us there could not help but get intoxicated by the astronomer's excitement. For the next four hours, until three in the morning, we enjoyed the celestial viewing amongst new and old friends.

Venus, the "goddess of love and beauty" moved in front of the sun, but real love and beauty were right here in the outskirts of Barrow. To think that, twenty-five years ago, fear had almost made us turn around and miss out on meeting these warm and most generous Inupiat people.

STRENGTH TO YOUR SWORD ARM

I WAS BROUGHT UP shaking hands. Along with the basic "please" and "thank you," it was considered respectful to offer the right hand and make eye contact when meeting, greeting, or congratulating someone. The way a hand was shaken, we were told, reveals one's character.

I remember my grandfather, tall and stocky with hands as big as shovels. I remember how he used to offer his glue-smeared fingers with the dark-rimmed nails to confirm an order of leather or nails for his shoe-making business in Switzerland. I can still smell the leather and hear the salesman's and Grandpa's agreeing laughter while they shook hands to seal a deal. That handshake was as good as an authorized purchase order or as good as a signature.

When I moved to Canada, I found it bizarre that shaking hands, especially among women, is not common. People meet with simply a nod and perfunctory words like: "Nice to meet you," and, a few moments later, they part with: "Nice meeting you."

Sometimes, I find myself standing in a group of men who shake each others' hands but offer me nothing more than a nod. Am I less worthy of a handshake because I am a woman?

Last week, my husband and I entered a sports-bar. As we searched for an empty table, my husband recognized a business acquaintance. The two men greeted each other with a heartfelt double shake, reinforcing the courtesy by putting the left hand over the knot of shaking hands.

My husband introduced me, "This is my wife, Verena."

The man, not offering his hand to me, said, "Pleased to . . .," and faced my husband while finishing, " . . . meet you." Without taking a fresh breath he continued, "I'm only passing through town. I'll give you a call next time I'm in the area, and we can get together over lunch."

There we stood, a trio surrounded by the murmur of laughing patrons and the smell of french-fries and finger-food. Totally ignoring me, my husband and his acquaintance eyed the oversized TV screen that showed a discussion over the 2004/2005 cancelled NHL season. They joyfully speculated on all the winter's free evenings ahead and agreed on the tasty food in this place. As they said their adieus—with another handshake—my husband's business acquaintance turned to me, "Nice meeting you."

How does he know if it was nice to meet me or not?

I stretched out my arm. He looked at my hand, then at me and with a patronizing smile, he took my hand.

I gave it all I had.

His touch felt sweaty and limp like a damp washcloth. He retrieved his hand and shook it loose. Then he finally looked into my face.

"Wow, that's quite a handshake."

With a satisfied grin that I felt all the way down to my belly I said, "Nice meeting you."

I realize that different countries have different customs. In some cultures, people embrace, kiss each other's cheeks, bow, rub noses, or tilt their Stetsons. We, men and women of Europe and North America with manners, I assumed, shake hands.

Handshaking became popular during the middle ages in Europe. It is believed that warriors, when meeting their opponents in peace times, stretched out their right hand—their sword arm—to show friendliness and to prove the hand was without weapons.

This brings me back to my belief that a handshake is a symbol of a person's character. I speculate that Donald Trump agrees with my view, that he has his distinctive reasons for shaking some of his contestants' hands on the TV show *The Apprentice*.

A few days ago, I found another ally in an unlikely place. While visiting Vancouver, I walked into a beauty salon hoping that a hairdresser could squeeze me in between appointments and help me with my bad hair day. I was introduced to Keith, who approached me with a warm smile, made eye contact and said, "Pleased to meet you. What can I do for you today?" He shook my hand—firmly.

I blurted out, "I like your handshake."

"Thank you," Keith said, "I hate nothing more than a handshake that feels like a wet noodle."

Maybe there is hope after all.

First published in *Daytripping*

FOREST FIRES

WITH THE STEAMING cup of coffee, my early morning indulgence, I open the door to my balcony and am taken aback—by smoke.

We are not metropolitan enough for smog, but we are rural enough for smoke. Two days ago I heard water bombers—a sure sign of serious fires. Three hundred kilometers west, near Anahim Lake, ten thousand hectares of forest are burnt—nature's way of spring cleaning?

Depending on the wind, eventually dark, plume clouds crawl into town.

The thick air smells sour. I close the door and settle at the kitchen nook. It will be an inside day for me today, no chatting with Bob the squirrel who runs along the telephone wire every day. No shopping. I don't want to end up with a migraine.

Unless the prime minister visits, TV reporters and camera people seldom make the long trip to the central interior of British Columbia.

The *Williams Lake Tribune* publishes twice a week, so we rely on the radio and the "bush telephone" (gossip) to find out details. Sometimes fear makes rumours grow faster than a fire can spread.

I refill my favourite cup—a gift from a local potter—and tune into our radio station. Anahim Lake's evacuation notice has been lifted.

Throughout our Cariboo—Chilcotin region, beetle-killed pine trees stand with their red needles, like matches, ready to burst into flames. Even though we have a couple of manned watch towers left, some predict that one day, a fire will burn over the hills and into town—an unthinkable possibility.

Most of us have a plan, or some boxes packed.

Last week, my son signed the mortgage for his first home, a fixer-upper with thirsty wood-siding on a romantic, treed property. His well only produces two gallons of water a minute. If his backyard starts to burn all he can do is run and hope that the road out is not blocked by the blaze.

Our home is beside the main road through town—Highway 97. If one ignorant traveler throws a cigarette butt out of the car window, the bone-dry ditch catches fire. Even a piece of discarded glass, combined with the heat of the sun can ignite the yellow grass.

My writing pal, whose property borders crown land, has sprinklers sitting on her roof. My friend, a rancher, worries not only about house and men, but also about how fast her family will be able to open the gates so the cows can run for their lives.

The bear I saw during my walk in the woods four days ago gave me weak knees, but the thought of how many animals won't outrun this year's forest fires, turns my stomach.

As I place my cup in the dishwasher, I listen to the tale-end of the local news.

We will be in for a spectacular show of lightning and thunder tonight. The rain, thick and acid, will depress the smoke and ash and cool off the heat. But will the atmospheric electricity start new fires?

The flip side—and there is always a flip side—is the jobs forest fires create. It is no secret that our students stand in line for work with the well-trained fire response team. The physically demanding and dangerous jobs pay very well.

Also, nature recuperates. Morels are known to grow like weeds on one-year-old scorched earth.

Still, one might think, why don't we move away from this fire-hazardous area? I guess the same reason, Vancouverites, including our daughter, live in Vancouver, despite the possibilities of an earthquake. We stay because it's our home; it's where our neighbours and friends became family.

For me, it's here, where, in a couple days, I will again sit on the balcony, telling Bob how lucky we are to live where we do, surrounded by nature, most times at its best.

First published in *Our Canada*

NOT READY FOR GRANDMOTHERHOOD

CONSIDERING MY TRACK record, it was a miracle they asked me to babysit.

My son and his girlfriend drove up our lane, their little Golf heavy laden with suitcases and sleeping-bags, with dishes, food, pillows, toys, and a list of instructions. The one-year-old Black Lab lay in Allison's arms like a baby.

Oliver and Allison were taking a one-week spring break to drive the six thousand kilometer round-trip from Williams Lake to Los Angeles and back. They had secured two tickets for "The Price is Right" with Bill Barker, whose retirement, after hosting the US game show for thirty-five years, had been announced earlier in the year of 2007.

Ever since watching the show as a child, Allison had wanted to see the host live, have a chance to be called up on stage as a contestant. She had tears in her eyes when she handed me the puppy. "Thank you so much for looking after her, Verena."

"We'll be fine," I said, hoping to sound convincing.

Giddy with excitement, Allison waved her arms through the opened passenger window, while Kenya scrambled to jump from my grip. Oliver honked the horn as the back-end of their car disappeared around the corner late Friday afternoon.

"Okay, my best friend, it's you and me," I said, carrying Kenya to the fenced backyard. "You're going to be a good girl, right?" I said it pleadingly, worried about possible worst case scenarios: her running off, getting lost, or heaven forbid, being run over by a car. Then immediately I consoled myself with positive thoughts, surrounding us and the house in white light.

My stress was, as Willy would judge, self-inflicted, fabricated anxiety. But I regarded this week of babysitting as my test to be a grandmother one day. Failure was not an option. Willy's main concern, on the other hand, was purely and concretely materialistic, our new birch flooring in the living room.

That wooden surface, or better, the perfect preservation of it, was Willy's one and only unbendable stipulation in letting Kenya stay with us. That Lab was not allowed inside the house. The issue had resolved itself when Oliver and Allison made it clear, Kenya was an outside dog. Therefore, she slept on her pillow on the balcony.

The next morning, I was up at six because my previous dogs were early risers and because I had been awake with worries half the night. When I peeked through the window, Kenya was curled up peacefully on her bed, asleep.

After drinking my first, relaxing cup of coffee I opened the door. The puppy lazily stretched her limbs and looked at me with sleepy eyes as if asking, "What's up, new friend?" I fed her breakfast and loaded her in the back of my SUV.

Two blocks later, I smelled her regurgitated food. *My own fault. I should have known better.* By the time I parked the car at the head of our River Valley Trail and let Kenya out, the accident was cleanly licked up.

Descending the graveled trail, I cleared my nostrils from the car's malodor, inhaling deeply the scent of grassland and fir trees while the puppy ran circles around me.

"Good girl," I praised. "You'll be nice and tired for the rest of the day."

She listened to me, more or less, until we encountered another dog and its owner. The second the woman spotted us, she protectively lifted her pooch into her arms. The real danger, however, was not Kenya, but that look she threw at me.

Mumbling, "I'm just the babysitter," I took hold of Kenya's collar, tied it to the leash and pulled her away. A few minutes later, I let her run free again. We crossed a bridge, paused for the dog to gulp some creek water, continued climbing to the other side of the valley, and looping back to the car without further troubles.

At home, as I unlocked the front door, the phone rang. It was Oliver. He and Allison were in Eugene, Oregon, where they planned to spend the rest of the day and the night. I told them what an angel Kenya was.

Later in the afternoon I checked, for the umptieth time, on the puppy through my kitchen window. My eyes got diverted to a commotion on the road. My stomach jumped to my throat when I spotted a lifeless dog lying on the pavement. Déjà vu of Ally, our road-killed Heinz 57, raced through my brain as I rushed onto the balcony.

Kenya was not the dog on the road. But she was a spectator through the railing.

People ran hysterically to the dead animal. The men from the house across the street lifted the limp canine up and carried it over onto their lawn. The woman brought a blanket and covered up the corpse.

Convinced that Kenya must be traumatized, I lured her into the backyard and played catch. The way she chased the ball and wagged her tail made it clear, her psychological state was better than mine. I left her and went back to my duties in the house.

The next time I checked on her, she was gone. I called her name—nothing. I yelled—nothing. Again my stomach crept upwards. Then I saw her. My son and his girlfriend's treasure that they had entrusted me to look after and protect stood outside the fence, on the side of the busy road, looking at me with innocent eyes.

Now what? Kenya needed to be locked up on the patio or tied up in the backyard. Since Lady, one of my other previous dogs, had hanged herself on a rope, tying any other animal to a chain was out of the question. So onto the balcony Kenya went with her toys and water dish. "We can do this," I encouraged, "not to worry."

I hoped the dog believed me, for I was not convinced. This watch over Oliver and Allison's "baby" turned out to be much harder than anticipated.

At eight o'clock on Tuesday evening, a text message from the kids arrived. "Standing in line at the Hollywood complex."

The show was scheduled for the following day. Their reason for having packed the sleeping bags dawned on me. My guess was they would not get a good night's sleep.

For me though, the nights and daybreaks were the least nerve-racking hours. I stretched out my coffee-and-breakfast-session each morning before opening the balcony door, until by Wednesday, I had waited too long.

When I finally opened the kitchen door, the balcony's acrylic painted floor was littered with white fluff. Kenya's pillow lay frayed with a gaping hole in one corner. The culprit, hiding under the picnic table, looked at me guiltily.

"Poor puppy," I said, slowly approaching her, "it's Grandma's fault for leaving you until you're bored." "Oops, did I really say that? Grandma?"

I changed our schedule, alternated the pup's time from the balcony to—against my better judgement—the backyard, carefully choosing trees and rope length. I walked Kenya, or better, she walked me, twice a day, double the distance. My joints were sore and my toes blistered. White fibrefill was scattered throughout the yard and balcony. I purchased more toys and another cushion. My plan was to throw the chewed ones out by the end of the week.

The work in my office was piling up. My husband rolled his eyes at the frozen dinners. Overall, though, things were still going well. Kenya was alive and happy.

We hadn't heard from the kids in two days. No news must be good news. Surely, Oliver and Allison's custom printed T-shirts with the slogan, "I want to be the next Bob Barker," created enough attention for them to be brought onto the stage. Possibly, they might have won teak furniture, a crimson convertible, or better yet, loads of cash.

In the meantime, my grandmother confidence was crumbling. Despite my measuring and plotting, I was running out of trees to tie Kenya to: From one she had reached the shed where she scratched the door, from another, the fence, where she ripped out boards, and from yet another tree, she dug out and gnawed at the underground sprinkler. Where the nozzle was, frazzled and torn wires stuck out. When, in a couple of weeks, the automatic watering system will be turned on and found faulty, and my husband will wonder what happened, I intend to play ignorant.

By Friday, Kenya had attacked the patio furniture. I considered getting my hands on sleeping pills—for me and the dog. But I persevered without drugs, continued walking, cleaning, worrying, and praying.

Finally, Sunday arrived. As Oliver and Allison's Golf came up our driveway, I called Kenya. She bolted past me, through the open kitchen door, into the living room, where she excitedly piddled on the floor. The kids in the meantime had come in through the front door. While jumping up at them, Kenya slid and slipped, trying in vain to get a grip with her claws on the varnish-smooth wood flooring. The more we screamed, the more the frightened dog peed.

Kenya and all of us—I after mopping up—retreated onto the balcony. Sitting around the picnic-table, we learned that, even though Oliver and Allison had spent an uncomfortable night in the line-up to get a front seat, and regardless of their T-shirt investment, they had not been called onto the stage of "The Price Is Right." They didn't meet Bob Barker nor win valuables or money.

I thought, "We all had our losses," and hoped Oliver wouldn't notice the chewed patio chair legs. "And we had our wins." Mine was counting my blessings over Kenya being a canine and not a grandchild, Oliver and Allison's to get their puppy back alive.

WRITES TO LIFE

I USED TO SELL them with pride and joy. I used to envy the customers who could afford the deluxe models. In the stationery store, where I worked when I was young, before my hands were speckled with liver spots, we displayed fountain pens, priced from nine ninety-five, packaged in blister packs, to eight hundred dollars, displayed on satin-lined shelves under a glass counter. As the prices differed, so did the customers.

Students didn't care about fit or nib. They usually selected a mandarin-orange plastic casing with a cheap steel nib and matched it with a box of purple or green ink cartridges.

For a teacher, his or her fountain pen was the tool to grade papers. A smooth and unimpeded red flow was essential—a prototype adequate.

Artists and writers, recognizable by their attire, were a different lot. They insisted on testing many pens of all price ranges while chatting in great length about their projects they were working on. After considerable time had passed, they gave me a reverie smile, "Thank you. I'll think about it."

I particularly liked serving the eager, well-dressed executive who, I assumed, came straight from his board meeting, where he had been the recipient of a promotion. His fountain pen had to feel like an extension of his hand, long and lean, or broad and burly. The nib, preferably a flexible gold nib, needed to be perfectly aligned with the angle of his hand to the paper. With longing, I watched as the ambitious young customer wrote on our carefully selected cotton-fibre paper. Mostly they tested signing, which fascinated me for I looked at people's signature as their self-portrait.

Physicians also took great care in selecting their pen. I doubt it affected the readability of prescriptions in any way. Reaching for one of the velvet cases and preparing an ebony lacquered gem for testing, I felt the urge to wear white gloves. Once, serving a handsome doctor, I imagined the clip, which was shaped like an arrow, leap from the pen and shoot straight through my heart. When that doctor purchased the fountain pen, I contemplated—for a moment or two—offering him, as a package deal with the fountain pen, myself for marriage.

Once the customers left, I cleaned the beauties, holding the unscrewed bottom halves of the casings under the flow of warm water, inhaling the aroma of the pure ink. The first dark, then lighter fluid emanated over my hands and disappeared down the drain. And with it my hope of owning a gold-nibbed fountain pen.

Thirty-five years later, a writer now, I am still fantasizing about fountain pens. I picture my hand guiding an elegant pen with a wide-point nib over the paper, transforming my ideas into fiction. The muse at work—success in progress.

A week ago, I went into our new super-sized office and computer supply store in Williams Lake. (Sooner or later, even rural communities join the twenty-first century.) Strolling along the display counter, I spotted a fountain pen, lying like a priceless piece of jewellery, on a soft white cushion. My heart must have missed a beat or two as I leaned closer to the glass. The price was one-hundred and ninety-nine dollars—promising. The nib looked gold.

I asked the girl, whose name tag indicated "Customer Assistant," "Can I test this pen?"

"Huh? Test the pen?" she said with a bored frown on her face.

"Yes, try it out. Can I hold it, write with it?"

"I'll get someone else," she offered, brushing her long hair momentarily out of her face. A few feet away she nabbed another clerk who was busy typing on a keyboard. She gestured into my direction. I waited with mounting ardour until the obviously important task at the computer was finished. Finally, the "Assistant Manager" faced me from behind the counter.

"You want to *test* this pen?"

"Yes, please," I said, "I would like to see how it fits in my hand and glides on the paper."

He lifted up the fountain pen as if it was a dinosaur bone. His soon sweaty fingers fondled the pen for a few minutes, but he failed to compute its mechanics. He asked me politely—I have to give him that—to wait while he fetched the manager.

The groomed, very young manager informed me, while placing his Palm Pilot on the counter, "Fountain pens cannot be tested."

Reading his name tag, I said, "Taylor," paused for effect, then instructed in a motherly voice, "fountain pens need to be tested."

The child-manager thought it his duty to enlighten me. "You see, once the cartridge seal is broken, the ink flows freely and steadily through the nib here." He pointed to the nib. "Its current can't be stopped and will therefore flood the case and consequently our display."

The juvenile look he gave me seemed to say, "That's the way it is."

I toyed with the idea of setting him straight. But then, instead, I burst out laughing.

I guess my liver spotted hands are not my only signs of age. Besides, he saved me from saying, "Thank you. I'll think about it."

EGG WAR WITH A
DAB OF AROMAT

"EIERTUETSCHLE" IS an Easter tradition from the old country, one of the few that our kids don't embarrassingly denounce.

Years ago, when the children were small enough to be excited about doing crafts, we gathered grasses and leaves from the garden or the bush along our driveway. Back inside, we wrapped them around raw eggs, gently fastening the artwork with twine. These concoctions we boiled in water with lots of onion-peels. The results were hard-boiled eggs in different shades of brown with intricate designs of streaks and leaves.

Now, like most Canadians, we use food-colours.

We don't hide our Easter eggs in the backyard. Instead, I display them in a grass-green wood shavings-filled basket along with Lindt Swiss chocolates. In the center, where you would expect a chocolate bunny, I put our treasured yellow-red little canister of Aromat, the Swiss seasoning salt that is a mixture of MSG (Monosodium glutamate), hardened fats and oils, and other spices.

We are ready for our egg competition, the tradition we call "Tuetschle."

Let me explain. "Tuetschle" derives from the word "Tutsch," which means bump or collision. Adding the letters "i" and "e" belittles—in a cute way—the main word "tutsch." Therefore "Tuetschle" is a little, cute, gentle knock.

The Swiss have a habit of adding "i" and "e" to their words. Maybe they feel the need to make things small scale, because their country is so tiny.

Make no mistake though that there is nothing tiny about "Tuetschle." It is not just a friendly game. It's a competition. It's serious business. In our family, everyone remembers who last year's champion was.

Each participant, who is brave enough to enter the contest, chooses an egg. Two players, or should I say "Egg-Tuetschle-Athletes," hold their egg so the narrower end, the head, is exposed. They then initiate contact by Tuetschle, exquisite combating egg-head to egg-head.

Never—and here comes a scientific fact—will both eggshells crack simultaneously. One shell will crack consequently to the first more or less gentle hit. There will be loud booing and cheering from the crowd around the table. The broken egg and pride-injured contestant will still have a chance to redeem himself as the pair of eggs come into "bum" to "bum" conflict. Sometimes the winning egg breaks, probably "cracking" under the tremendous pressure to perform. If this occurs, it will get the whole family going, chanting for one or the other jock or egg. The finale follows: unbroken "head" against unbroken "bum."

The loser peels his or her egg and eats it with a dab of Aromat. You may substitute salt, but really, Aromat is it. The winner goes onto the next round.

Without naming any names, I will tell you of some of the cheaters we have in this family, just in case you might want to try this competition at your house.

Watch for the person with the biggest hands—in our family it's the former butcher—protecting the whole egg in his giant palm. Not fair.

One rival withdraws his egg at the last second so that the "hitter" bangs his prized possession on the table. Not funny.

Another offender suffers under the delusion that an immensely hard hit might increase her odds. Not true.

And finally, there is the player who fights a psychological warfare. She will look you in the eye and say, "You know you're going to lose," and hit. This is unfortunately true, but not fair nor funny.

One year, a grand champion egg emerged. It just could not be broken. Upon further inspection, we found that this blue egg was made of onyx. That player won first prize in cheating, but is now disqualified from the competition for life. He's lucky to be let into the house around Easter time.

I am unsure of where this tradition came from, but I am certain of where it's going. Everybody and anybody who ever spent Easter brunch at our table is introduced to "Eier Tuetschle."

Oliver's girlfriend studied the rules, hijacked one of my Aromat containers and started a tradition with her family in Vancouver, even though she only eats the boiled egg white and hands the yolk to Oliver.

The first time Melanie's Irish boyfriend, Damien, sat at our table for Easter brunch, I couldn't read his thoughts. Either he was thoroughly amused or thought we are a bunch of crackheads. But he participated bravely and put on his big smile, even though he passes on the egg white to Melanie, eating only the yolk with a generous Aromat sprinkle. Clearly, he humors us because he wants to remain in good standing with our family for he has fallen in love with Aromat.

Farm Gates

WITH MY ARMS leaning on the steering wheel, I sit and stare at the shut gate.

I could turn around. Susie doesn't know I'm coming. On the other hand, it would be a shame to let the birthday card and the tin can with my home-baked cookies go to waste.

Usually, the forty-minute drive to my friend's house is a relaxing respite from work in town, especially once I turn off Horsefly Road onto the Wildflower Ranch's mile long, gravel-and-dirt driveway. I roll down my window, inhale the fresh country air and, anticipating each cattle-guard, advance in first gear.

"It is late July," I thought just a moment ago, "if I'm lucky, I might see a deer, a fox, or an eagle." Instead, I find myself in front of this shut gate.

Still undecided, I look around. To my right, half a dozen or so cows forage in deep grass. To my left, pine trees stand surrounded by lush underbrush, blooming fireweed, daisies, and Indian paintbrush. On the other side of the gate, a palette of yellow and green separate irrigated and nonirrigated fields.

With a sigh, I get out. I know this gate is going to be trouble. Six strands of barbed wires, with long narrow sticks woven in, stretch across the path. A ten-inch long piece of wood is wedged between the gate-post and the top wire.

I try, with my index finger and thumb, to wiggle it loose. It is as stiff as a frozen steak. From my Jetta, I fetch my garden mitts that I keep handy to fill up my diesel tank, pull them on, and try again, banging at the piece of wood with the strength of my whole hand and then my arm. I try to kick it with my foot, but either the latch is too high or my legs too short. I lean into it with my upper body.

Suddenly, the raw, wooden peg dislodges; wires and sticks fall to the ground. "Ha!" I gloat, "Gotcha!" dragging the wobbly gate to the side.

I drive through and stop again.

I hate gates. Had I known about this one, I might have invited one of my friends to come along. Then it would have been the passenger's job—an old Western custom—to open the gate.

Susie will laugh at my "problem." The last few years, her family has faced enormous ranching challenges: the recent BSE scare, dropping cattle prices, and uncooperative haying weather. Because of their efficiently run operation and innovative spirit to try new things, such as tap into the "homegrown" food market, they are one of the few, still actively operating ranches.

Refocusing on my problem at hand, I pick up the prickly wires and stretch the flimsy roadblock enough to stick the last piece of lumber in the gate-frame's bottom loop. Then I pull at the top, pull and pull some more, trying for the wooden hook to meet the loop. I am off by more than a foot.

Then, of course, it starts to rain. I hadn't noticed dark clouds moving in. *What if I speed to the ranch house, drop off the gift and return immediately?* I look at the cows, estimating how long it would take them to escape. What if I block the opening by parking the car sideways and then make my way by foot? Whatever I do, the problem that sooner or later I will have to shut this gate, remains.

It's pouring now. Rainwater seeps down my neck. Giving the strands of barbed wires one more serious pull, I trip and fall onto the wet ground. The pole slips from my gloved hand, bounces, and scratches my face. Getting up, I shake muddy water from my jacket, feeling myself blushing. With nobody around, I am still embarrassed.

"It's not funny," I say to the one brown cow placidly watching me as she chews. Once more, I pick up the wires. A barb stabs through the wet glove into my palm. I channel my pain and frustration into one mighty shove—and the piece of wood wedges into place.

Soaking wet, I slump onto the driver's seat and proceed to the house.

"Mom's not here," Susie's teenaged son says. "She should be back soon." He looks me up and down, "Man, you look whipped."

"Never mind," I say already rushing back to my mud-splashed Jetta, realizing that if I get to the gate before Susie does, I can wait for her there, and she can deal with the blasted thing.

Typically for the Cariboo, the rain has stopped as quickly as it started. The sun is out again by the time I stop in front of the barricade. Instead of Susie, though, there stands a female moose, majestic and beautiful.

I turn off the engine and watch. Lifting her right front leg, then her left, the big cow steps over the fence beside the gate as if it were an obstacle at a miniature golf course. I roll down the window for a better view and she responds by moving her long head, with the flap of fur hanging from her throat, toward me.

For a moment we look at each other. Then the moose turns her head and unhurriedly strolls into the pine trees. The massive pale-brown animal looks surprisingly slender from behind. Within seconds, she blends into the woods and disappears, stubby tail and all.

I take a deep breath. For the first time that day, I smell the ripe grass mixed with the scent of cattle and wild flowers. Even though it's Susie's birthday, I end up getting the best present.

How lucky, the gate was closed.

First published in *Farm & Ranch Living*

I Am a Writer

I LOVED — MOST mornings—getting out of bed, anticipating easy, breezy days, as a stay-at-home mom.

Call me old fashioned, but seeing my husband off to work and our two kids, with healthy lunches in their backpacks, to the school bus on time, gave me pleasure. I took pride keeping our, although modest, home clean and comfortable. "Work", for me, was vacuuming the rugs and cleaning windows, because I disliked these chores. Otherwise, being a homemaker was a picnic.

Laundry day for me was a day of slacking. Once the washing machine and dryer did the hard work, I only stretched the spring-fresh smelling sheets over the beds; folded stain-removed, clean sportswear; and hung ironed and starched shirts evenly spaced in the walk-in closet.

Walking our dog was my free outdoor gym time, often with the bonus of seeing a deer or a fox. Bargain hunting during grocery shopping was shamefully gratifying. Cooking up new recipes and filling the house with aroma of spices and sauces gave me a cheery buzz, especially when Willy and the kids devoured my dinners with smiling faces.

Reconciling bank statements to the cent was so rewarding, it should have been illegal.

It was my pride and joy to be involved in our children's activities, to drive them to and from soccer games and piano lessons, and to help them study.

"I hate math," Oliver would say.

"That's why it's called home 'work.'"

"When I grow up," Melanie predicted, "I'll be a housewife. Then I don't have to work."

Not only did I almost believe this myself, her prejudice is shared by the broad public.

When asked, while accompanying my husband during his Real Estate Conventions, what I did, I learned that most think of homemakers as highly as they do of lost customers. That's why this one time I tried to impress a realtor by mentioning what I considered my real "work."

"I vacuum and clean windows," I said.

The instant dismissal showed on his face. Realizing, I was not handing out or receiving business cards, the realtor performed a one-hundred-and-eighty-degree turn on his heels, and without another word, left me standing there.

Desperate for respect, I have, over the years, attempted different approaches.

"I am a caterer."

"Oh really? Do you do conventions, weddings, and funerals?"

"I might one day. My kids are not married yet and my husband is still alive."

One-hundred-and-eighty-degree turn.

"I do bookkeeping and payroll."

"Interesting. What company do you work for?"

"It's not a company per se. I work at home. One payroll in the near future." *Once we have enough money to pay myself.*

One-hundred-and-eighty-degree turn.

It's not just at conventions I experience this alienation. It happens practically at every adult-oriented gathering, where we meet new people. Once at a Christmas dinner, I was loudly judged the "prettiest housewife at this table."

In any case, my days were numbered. Being in that liberating space between moved-out kids and no-grandchildren-yet, I was going to have to find a new occupation, a real job, possibly one that I didn't love so much.

"You always liked to write," my husband encouraged. "Why don't you put together a few stories and see what happens?"

So I did. I wrote a slice-of-life article on how a mother feels when children leave home, submitted it, and promptly got it published in the *Vancouver Province*. That was easy—as easy, breezy as being a homemaker.

With a rather guilty feeling, because this writing thing was too much fun to be considered work, I decided to become a writer. And at the next get-together, I proudly said to the first person who asked about my occupation, "I am a writer."

"Oh really?"

Wow. I got somebody's attention. I beamed, "Yes, really."

"Do you have a published book?"

I felt turning red. "Hmm, not yet, but I have published stories."

"So you have a column?"

"Not exactly."

"Oh." Pause. "Nice talking to you."

"I love my life," I said to her back.

I don't think she heard me, or rather, I don't think she was interested in listening. But I should thank her, for she gave me my "aha moment."

Validation for what I do, I realized, can't come from other people, it comes from within. Because I love what I do, it makes me not unworthy, but lucky.

Ultimately, there is not that much difference from being a writer to being a homemaker. Editors or fellow writers run their pens—my writers group friends know not to use red—over clean double-spaced pages, like a muddy dog romps over a white carpet. Final edits are as pleasurable as vacuuming, but—reading a published story is as satisfying as Christmas dinner with everybody home.

During the last seven years, I have received more rejections than I have done loads of washes in twenty years, I think. True, I have sold a few stories, mostly to magazines, which compensate a writer with a free copy. On the satisfactory scale it compares to "thank you for the clean socks in my drawer" from my husband.

Most importantly, I am happy to get out of bed in the morning and step into the office—after the house is cleaned and the laundry done—curious as to what my fingers will produce.

Who knows, I might even write a book one day.

Acknowledgment

I would like to thank the few people who never doubted that I am a writer.

Donna Milner, I can't begin to tell you how much I appreciate our countless walks and talks, your guidance, the time you gave me and this project. Only with you can I sit and discuss one sentence for a full hour and enjoy it.

Maegi Schlaepfer, my beloved sister, I extend my heartfelt gratitude for your persistence in practicing English so that—I quote: "I can read and understand your book when it is in print." What better motivation could I have had?

I would also like to thank you, my dear friend Elke Schneider, for the open ears during our tea time, the loving encouragement and eagle-eyed grammar check.

Thank you, Joyce Aaltonen for always laughing at the right spots when listening to my readings and Ann Walsh for all the writing doors you continue to open for me.

To my family, who is my world, I say: Thank you Oliver, for the screen saver on my computer: "Just Write Man!" Thank you Melanie, for your one trillion "You can do it, Mami." Thank you Willy, for always saying, "Go for it," and never asking, "How much did you write today?" I love you more today than yesterday.

CPSIA information can be obtained at www.ICGtesting.com
Printed in the USA
LVOW040251120612

285623LV00001BA/15/P